Charles Yatman

Temple songs

Charles Yatman

Temple songs

ISBN/EAN: 9783337266387

Printed in Europe, USA, Canada, Australia, Japan

Cover: Foto ©Thomas Meinert / pixelio.de

More available books at **www.hansebooks.com**

TEMPLE SONGS

SELECTED BY

CHARLES H. YATMAN.

MUSICAL EDITORS:

JNO. R. SWENEY AND WM. J. KIRKPATRICK.

———————

PHILADELPHIA:

Published by JOHN J. HOOD, 1018 Arch St.

TEMPLE · SONGS

Hide Thou Me.

FANNY J. CROSBY.   "Thou art my hiding place."—Ps. xxxii. 7.   ROBERT LOWRY. By per.

1. In thy cleft, O Rock of a - ges, Hide thou me; When the fitful tempest
2. From the snare of sinful pleasure, Hide thou me; Thou, my soul's eternal
3. In the lonely night of sorrow, Hide thou me; Till in glory dawns the

ra - ges, Hide thou me; Where no mortal arm can sev - er From my
trea - sure, Hide thou me; When the world its power is wielding, And my
mor - row, Hide thou me; In the sight of Jordan's bil-low, Let thy

heart thy love forev - er, Hide me, O thou Rock of a - ges, Safe in thee.
heart is almost yielding, Hide me, O thou Rock of a - ges, Safe in thee.
bo-som be my pillow; Hide me, O thou Rock of a - ges, Safe in thee.

Jesus is Good to Me.

Rev. E. H. Stokes. D. D.

Jno. R. Sweney.

1. I love my Saviour, his heart is good, He has loved me o'er and o'er;
2. He calls, I rise, and he maketh me whole,—How fond his tender embrace!
3. I want to love him with all my heart, Tho' all its powers are small;
4. He's good to me in my sorrow's night, He's good in the tempest's roll;

He sought me wand'ring, I'm saved by his blood, And I love him more and more.
He cleanses and keeps me and blesses my soul'—My day the smile of his face.
I will not keep from him any part, For he is worthy of all.
He bringeth from darkness into light,—With joy he filleth my soul.

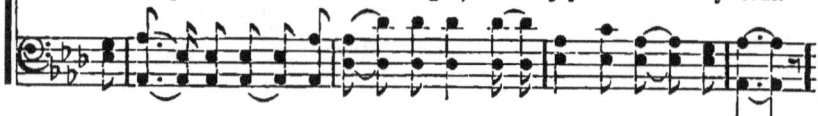

CHORUS.

Je - sus is good to me, . . . Je - sus is good to me; . . .

to me,

to me;

So good! so good! Je - sus is good to my soul.

Abiding.

Rev. E. H. Stokes, D.D.   Jno. R. Sweney.

1. My soul for light and love had earnest longings, Oh, how it longed for
2. Oh, how en-riching is this sacred treasure! En-riching to this
3. Oh, yes, I rest, how blessed is the rest-ing! I rest to-day, I'm

fellowship di-vine! I sought it here and there, I sought it ev'rywhere, At
soul, this soul of mine; There's nothing any where Can with this love compare, And
resting all the time; "Come," echoes thro' the air, "Come," and the resting share, And

CHORUS.

last, thro' faith, the holy boon was mine. I'm a-bid-ing, gracious
I henceforth, for-ev-er, Lord, am thine.
Je-sus will be yours as he is mine.

Sav-iour, I'm a-bid-ing in thy precious love to-day; I'm a-

bid-ing, yes, a-bid-ing In thy love, thy precious love, to-day.

DO RE MI FA SO LA SI

Behold the Bridegroom.

"And at midnight there was a cry made, Behold, the bridegroom cometh : go ye out to meet him."—Matt. xxv. 6.

R. E. H.

R. E. HUDSON.

1. Are you ready for the Bridegroom When he comes, when he comes? Are you
2. Have your lamps trimm'd and burning When he comes, when he comes; Have your
3. We will all go out to meet him When he comes, when he comes; We will
4. We will chant al·le·lu·ias When he comes, when he comes; We will

ready for the Bridegroom When he comes, when he comes, Behold! he cometh!
lamps trimm'd and burning When he comes, when he comes, He quickly cometh!
all go out to meet him When he comes, when he comes; He surely cometh!
chant al·le·lu·ias When he comes, when he comes; Lo! now he cometh!

D.S.—Behold! he cometh!

Fine.

be-hold! he cometh! Be robed and read-y, for the Bridegroom comes.
he quick-ly cometh, O soul, be read-y when the Bridegroom comes
he sure-ly cometh! We'll go to meet him when the Bridegroom comes
lo! now he cometh! Sing al·le·lu·ia! for the Bridegroom comes.

be-hold! he cometh! Be robed and read-y, for the Bridegroom comes.

CHORUS.

D.S.

Behold the Bridegroom, for he comes, for he comes!

Behold the Bridegroom, for he comes, for he comes

DO RE MI FA SO LA SI

Say, are You Ready?

A. S. KIEFFER. "Therefore be ye also ready."—Matt. xxiv. 44. **T. C. O'KANE.**

7

1. Should the death an - gel knock at thy cham - ber, In the still
2. Ma - ny sad spir - its now are de - part - ing In - to the
3. Ma - ny redeemed ones now are as - cend - ing In - to the

watch of to - night, Say, will your spir - it pass in - to torment,
world of des - pair; Ev - 'ry brief moment brings your doom nearer;
mansions of light; Je - sus is pleading, pa - tiently pleading,

CHORUS.

Or to the land of de - light? Say, are you read - y?
Sin - ner, O sin - ner, be - ware!
O let him save you to - night.

Oh, are you read - y If the death an - gel should call?
should call?

Say, are you read-y? Oh, are you read-y? Mercy stands waiting for all.

DO RE MI FA SO LA SI

Always Abounding.

"Always abounding in the work of the Lord."—1 Cor. xv. 58.

E. A. BARNES.   WM. J. KIRKPATRICK.

1. Be earnest, my brothers, in word and in deed, Be active in reaping and
2. Be ready, my brothers, his call to o-bey, In seeking the erring and
3. Be zealous, my brothers, the light to extend, And unto all nations the

sow- ing the seed; And thus in the vineyard, with Je-sus to lead, Be
show-ing the way; And thus as his servants, remem - ber, we pray, Be
gos- pel to send; And thus, till the harvest in glo - ry shall end, Be

REFRAIN.

always abounding in the work of the Lord. Be always abounding in the

work of the Lord, Be always abounding in the work of the Lord; Be earnest, be

active, re- lying on his word, Be always abounding in the work of the Lord.

One more Day.

FRANK GOULD.

JNO. R. SWENEY.

9

1. One more day its twilight brings, One more day its shadow flings; One sweet hour of grate-ful prayer, Calling to rest . . . from toil and care.

2. One more day of conflict passed, One more vic - t'ry gained at last; One sweet hour in praise to spend, While at a throne . . . of grace we bend.

3. One more day of reaping o'er, One more sheaf to crown our store; One sweet hour to bathe the soul Here in the streams . . of joy that roll.

4. Saviour, when as now we rest, Leaning, trust - ing on thy breast, We shall cross the nar - row sea Still may we sing, . . . inspired by thee:—

CHORUS.

One day near - - er the land of song, One day near - - er the white-robed throng; There at the gate they watch and wait For a meeting that shall last forever.

they watch and wait,

DO RE MI FA SO LA SI

Over There.

T. C. O'KANE.

1. O, think of a home over there, By the side of the river of light,
2. O, think of the friends over there, Who before us the journey have trod,
3. My Saviour is now over there, There my kindred and friends are at rest;
4. I'll soon be at home over there, For the end of my journey I see;

Over there,

Where the saints all immortal and fair, Are robed in their garments of white.
Of the songs that they breathe on the air, In their home in the palace of God.
Then away from my sorrow and care, Let me fly to the land of the blest.
Many dear to my heart, over there, Are watching and waiting for me.

Over there.

REFRAIN.

O- ver there, o- ver there, O, think of a home over there,
O- ver there, o- ver there, O, think of the friends over there,
O- ver there, o- ver there, My Saviour is now o- ver there,
O- ver there, o- ver there, I'll soon be at home over there,

Over there, over there, over there,

O- ver there, over there, over there, O, think of a home over there.
O- ver there, over there, over there, O, think of the friends over there.
O- ver there, over there, over there, My Saviour is now over there.
O- ver there, over there, over there, I'll soon be at home over there.

over there,

The Half was Never Told.

11

P. P. B.   "Behold, the half was not told."—Kings x. 7.   P. P. Bliss.

1. Re - peat the sto - ry o'er and o'er, Of grace so full and free;
2. Of peace I on - ly knew the name, Nor found my soul its rest
3. My high - est place is ly - ing low At my Redeem - er's feet;
4. And oh, what rapture will it be With all the host a - bove,

I love to hear it more and more, Since grace has res - cued me.
Un - til the sweet-voiced angel came To sooth my wea - ry breast.
No re - al joy in life I know, But in his ser - vice sweet.
To sing through all e - ter - ni - ty The won - ders of his love!

CHORUS.

The half was never told, The half was never told,
nev - er told,   nev - er told,

1. Of grace divine, so wonder-ful, The half was never told.
2. Of peace, etc.
3. Of joy, etc.
4. Of love, etc.
nev - er told.

By per. of the John Church Co.,

DO RE MI FA SO LA SI

12 Cast thy Bread upon the Waters.

1. Cast thy bread up-on the wa-ters, Ye who have but scant supply,
2. Cast thy bread up-on the wa-ters, Poor and weary, worn with care,—
3. Cast thy bread up-on the wa-ters, Ye who have a-bundant store;
4. Cast thy bread up-on the wa-ters, Far and wide your treasures strew,
5. Cast thy bread up-on the wa-ters, Waft it on with praying breath,

An-gel eyes will watch above it;— You shall find it by and by!
Oft-en sitting in the shadow, Have you not a crumb to spare?
It may float on man-y-a bil-low, It may strand on many-a shore;
Scat-ter it with willing fin-gers, Shout for joy to see it go!
In some distant, doubtful moment It may save a soul from death;

He who in his righteous balance Doth each human ac-tion weigh
Can you not to those around you Sing some lit-tle song of hope,
You may think it lost for-ev-er, But, as sure as God is true,
For if you do close-ly keep it, It will on-ly drag you down;
When you sleep in solemn silence, 'Neath the morn and evening dew,

Will your sac-ri-fice remem-ber, Will your loving deeds re-pay.
As you look with longing vision Thro' faith's mighty tel-e-scope?
In this life or in the oth-er, It will yet return to you.
If you love it more than Je-sus, It will keep you from your crown.
Stranger hands, which you have strengthened, May strew lilies over you.

Praise ye the Lord.

FANNY J. CROSBY.   WM. J. KIRKPATRICK.

1. Praise ye the Lord, the hope of our sal-va-tion; Praise ye the Lord, our
2 Praise ye the Lord, whose throne is everlasting; Praise ye the Lord, whose

CHO.—Praise ye the Lord, for good it is to praise him; O let the earth his

soul's a-bid-ing trust; Great are his works and wonderful his counsels;
gifts are ev-er new; Praise ye the Lord, whose tender mercy falleth

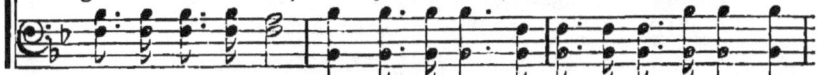

ma-jest-y proclaim; Shout, shout for joy and bow the knee before him;

Fine.

Praise ye the Lord, the only wise and just. Praise ye the Lord, our strength and our Re-
Pure as the rain and gentle as the dew. Praise ye the Lord, oh, glory! hal-le-

Sing to the harp and magnify his name.

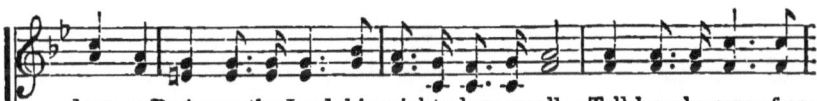

deemer, Praise ye the Lord, his mighty love recall,—Tell how he came from
lujah! Praise ye the Lord, whose kingdom has no end; Praise ye the Lord, who

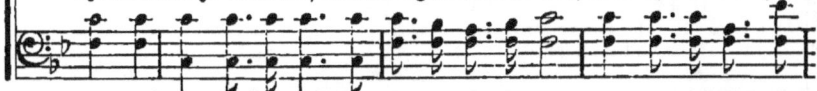

Chorus. D. C.

bondage to de-liv-er, Tell how he came to purchase life for   all.
watcheth o'er the faithful, Praise ye the Lord, our never changing Friend.

14 — Oh, the Joy that Awaits Me.

Geo. R. Clarke.   E. F. Miller.

1. Beyond the silent river,   In the glo - ry summer lands, In the
2. And when I cross that river,   The first I will a - dore; The
3. The next one who will greet me, In the mansions fair and bright, Will
4. Then cur - ly headed brother   And lit - tle ba - by dear, And

beautiful forever, Where the jeweled city stands, Where the ever blooming
first to bid me welcome, Up - on that golden shore, Will be my loving
be my sainted mother Arrayed in garments white, And then that gray-haired
bright eyed little sister, With merry laugh and cheer, They all will gather

flowers Send forth their sweet perfume, My heart's most loved and cherished
Saviour, The one who died for me, That in that long for - ev - er,
father, Close pressing by her side, Will grasp my hand with fervor
round me, To bid me welcome home, And watch with me the gath'ring

CHORUS.

In heavenly beauty bloom. Oh, the joy that there awaits me, When I
From sin I might be free.
Just o'er the swelling tide.
Of loved ones yet to come.

[no more!
reach that golden shore, When I grasp the hands of loved ones, To part with them

At the Golden Landing. 15

Edgar Page. Jno. R. Sweney.

1. Friends of yore have flown to heaven, Springing from the house of clay;
2. Oft-en at the shades of evening, When I sit me down to rest,
3. And I seem to see their fac-es, Beaming with ce-les-tial love,
4. And I think I hear them speaking, As they oft-en spake to me,
5. Broth-er, sis-ter, faithful sol-dier, If our mingling here so sweet,

Glad to gain their joy-ful free-dom, Borne by an-gel bands a-way.
One by one I count them o-ver, They who are in glo-ry blest.
Shin-ing as their blessed Mas-ter, White-robed, with the saints above.
While I seem to hear them say-ing, "Pil-grim, heaven is waiting thee."
What shall be our joy-ous rap-ture When we at the landing meet!

CHORUS.

While on Pisgah's mount I'm standing, Looking t'ward the vernal shore,

There I seem to see them banding, Just beside the Golden Landing,

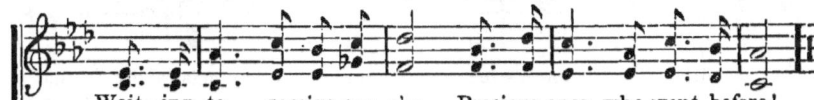

Wait-ing to receive me o'er, Precious ones who went before!

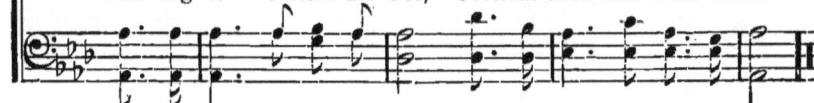

In the Morning.

Lizzie Edwards.　　　　　　　　　　　　　　　　Jno. R. Sweney.

1. We are pilgrims looking home, Sad and wea-ry oft we roam, But we
2. O these tender broken ties, How they dim our aching eyes, But like
3. When our fettered souls are free, Far beyond the narrow sea, And we
4. Thro' our pilgrim journey here, Tho' the night is sometimes drear, Let us

know 'twill all be well in the morning; When, our anchor firmly cast, Ev'ry
jewels they will shine in the morning; When our victor palms we bear, And our
hear the Saviour's voice in the morning; When our golden sheaves we bring To the
watch and persevere till the morning; Then our highest tribute raise For the

storm-y wave is past, And we gather safe at last in the morn-ing.
robes immor-tal wear, We shall know each other there, in the morn-ing.
feet of Christ our King, What a chorus we shall sing in the morn-ing.
love that crowns our days, And to Jesus give the praise in the morn-ing.

D. S.—sun-ny region bright, When we hail the blessed light of the morn-ing.

CHORUS.

When we all meet a-gain in the morn-ing, On the sweet blooming

D. S.

hills in the morn-ing; Nev-ermore to say good night In that

Cast thy Burden on the Lord. 17

W. J. K.

"Casting all your care upon him, for he careth for you."
1 Peter v. 7.

Wm. J. Kirkpatrick.

1. Wea-ry pil - grim on life's pathway, Struggling on beneath thy load,
2. Are thy tir - ed feet unstead - y? Does thy lamp no light af - ford?
3. Are the ties of friendship severed? Hushed the voices fond- ly heard?

Hear these words of con- so - la-tion,—"Cast thy bur - den on the Lord."
Is thy cross too great and hea - vy? Cast thy bur - den on the Lord.
Breaks thy heart with weight of anguish, Cast thy bur - den on the Lord.

CHORUS.

Cast thy bur-den on the Lord, Cast thy bur-den on the Lord, And he will

strengthen thee, sustain and comfort thee; Cast thy bur - den on the Lord.

4 Does thy heart with faintness falter?
Does thy mind forget his word?
Does thy strength succumb to weak-
Cast thy burden on the Lord. [ness?

5 He will hold thee up from falling,
He will guide thy steps aright;
He will strengthen each endeavor;
He will keep thee by his might.

Copyright, 1880, by John J. Hood.   *Temple Songs*-B

Wonderful Love of Jesus.

"The love of Christ, which passeth knowledge."
Eph. iii. 19.

E. D. Mund.　　　　　　　　　　　　　　　　E. S. Lorenz.

1. In vain in high and ho-ly lays My soul her grateful voice would raise; For
2. A joy by day, a peace by night, In storms a calm, in darkness light; In
3. My hope for pardon when I call, My trust for lift-ing when I fall; In

who can sing the worthy praise Of the won-derful love of Je-sus?
pain a balm, in weakness might, Is the won-derful love of Je-sus.
life, in death, my all in all, Is the won-derful love of Je-sus.

CHORUS.

Won-derful love! won-derful love! Won-der-ful love of Je-sus!

Wonder-ful love! won-derful love! Wonder-ful love of Je-sus!

From "Holy Voices," by per.

Are You Ready?

Mary D. James.

Jno. R. Sweney.

1. Should the summons, quickly fly - ing, On the slumb'ring nations fall,—
2. What if now the startling man - date Should the sleeping virgins hear,—
3. Is there oil in all your ves - sels? Are your garments pure and white?
4. Rise! ye vir - gins,—sleep no long - er,—Lest the call your souls surprise!

Lo! the heavenly Bridegroom com - eth, Would the sound your souls appal?
Are your lamps all trimm'd and burning? Should the Bridegroom now appear?
Are they wash'd in-the cleansing fountain, Fit to stand in Je - sus' sight?
Lest ye fail to meet the Bridegroom, When he cometh from the skies.

CHORUS.

Are you read - y? Are you read - y? Should you hear the midnight call?
Are you read - y? Are you read - y? Now to see your Lord ap - pear!
Are you read - y? Are you read - y? Are your lamps all clear and bright?
Oh, be read - y! Oh, be read - y! When he cometh from the skies;

Are you read - y? Are you read - y? Should you hear the midnight call?
Are you ready? Are you ready? Should you hear the midnight call? Should you hear the midnight call?
Are you read - y? Are you read - y? Now to see your Lord appear?
Are you ready? Are you ready? Now to see your Lord appear! Now to see your Lord ap - pear?
Are you read - y? Are you read - y? Are your lamps all clear and bright?
Are you ready? Are you ready? Are your lamps all clear and bright? Are your lamps all clear and bright?
Oh, be read - y! Oh, be read - y! Hasten, from your slumbers rise!
Oh, be ready! Oh, be ready! Hasten, from your slumbers rise! Hasten, from your slumbers rise!

DO KE MI FA SO LA SI

I Want to be a Worker.

I. B.　　　　　"The laborers are few."—Matt. ix. 27.　　　　　I. BALTZELL.

1. I want to be a worker for the Lord, I want to love and trust his holy
2. I want to be a worker ev-'ry day, I want to lead the erring in the
3. I want to be a worker strong and brave, I want to trust in Jesus' pow'r to
4. I want to be a worker; help me, Lord, To lead the lost and erring to thy

word; I want to sing and pray, and be bu-sy ev-'ry day In the
way That leads to heav'n above, where all is peace and love In the
save; All who will tru-ly come, shall find a hap-py home In the
word That points to joy on high, where pleasures never die In the

CHORUS.

1. vineyard of the Lord. I will work, I will pray, In the
2, 3, 4. kingdom of the Lord. I will work and pray, I will work and pray,

vineyard, in the vineyard of the Lord; of the Lord; I will work, I will

pray, I will la-bor ev-'ry day In the vineyard of the Lord.

DO RE MI FA SO LA

Help Just a Little.

Music from "The Wells of Salvation,"
new words by Rev. W. A. Spencer.

Wm. J. Kirkpatrick.

1. Brother for Christ's kingdom sighing, Help a lit-tle, help a lit-tle;
2. Is thy cup made sad by tri-al? Help a lit-tle, help a lit-tle;
3. Though no wealth to thee is giv-en, Help a lit-tle, help a lit-tle;

Help to save the mil-lions dy-ing, Help just a lit-tle.
Sweet-en it with self-de-ni-al, Help just a lit-tle.
Sac-ri-fice is gold in heav-en, Help just a lit-tle.

CHORUS.

Oh, the wrongs that we may righten! Oh, the hearts that we may lighten!

Oh, the skies that we may brighten! Helping just a lit-tle.

4 Let us live for one another,
    Help a little, help a little;
Help to lift each fallen brother,
    Help just a little.

5 Tho' thy life is pressed with sorrow,
    Help a little, help a little;
Bravely look t'ward God's to-morrow.
    Help just a little.

Sound the Battle Cry.

W. F. S.

Vigorously, in march time.

WM. F. SHERWIN. By per.

1. Sound the bat - tle cry, See! the foe is nigh; Raise the standard high
2. Strong to meet the foe, March-ing on we go, While our cause we know
3. Oh! thou God of all, Hear us when we call, Help us, one and all,

For the Lord; Gird your ar - mor on, Stand firm ev - 'ry one.
Must pre - vail; Shield and ban - ner bright, Gleam-ing in the light,
By thy grace; When the bat - tle's done, And the vic - t'ry won,

CHORUS.

Rest your cause up - on his ho - ly word. Rouse, then, sol- diers!
Bat - tling for the right, we ne'er can fail.
May we wear the crown be - fore thy face.

2d CHO.—*Rouse, then, freemen,*

ral - ly round the banner! Ready, stead-y, pass the word a-long; Onward,

come from hill and valley; Fathers, brothers, earnest, brave, and strong! Onward,

forward, shout a-loud, Ho-san- na! Christ is Captain of the migh- ty throng.

forward, all u- nit- ed ral - ly, " Death to Alchohol!" your bat -tle song.

Ye Must be Born Again.

"Verily, verily, I say unto thee, except a man be born again, he cannot see the kingdom of God."—John iii. 3.

W. T. SLEEPER.

GEO. C. STEBBINS. By per.

1. A rul - er once came to Jesus by night, To ask him the
2. Ye children of men, at - tend to the word So sol - emn - ly
3. O ye who would enter that glo - ri - ous rest, And sing with the
4. A dear one in heaven thy heart yearns to see, At the beauti - ful

way to salvation and light; The Master made answer in words true and plain, "Ye
uttered by Jesus the Lord, And let not this message to you be in vain, "Ye
ransomed the song of the blest; The life everlasting if ye would obtain, "Ye
gate may be watching for thee; Then list to the note of this solemn refrain, "Ye

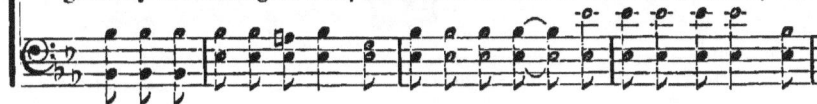

CHORUS.

must be born again." Ye must be born again, Ye must be born again,

again. again. again.

I ver - i - ly, ver - i - ly, say unto thee, Ye must be born again, again.

The New Song.

Flora L. Best.

Moderato.

Jno. R. Sweney.

1. There are songs of joy that I loved to sing, When my heart was as blithe as a
2. There are strains of home that are dear as life, And I list to them oft 'mid the

bird . . in spring; But the song I have learned is so full of cheer, That the
din . . of strife; But I know of a home that is wondrous fair, And I

CHORUS. Vivace.

dawn shines out in the darkness drear. O, the new, new song! O, the
sing the psalm they are singing there. O, the new, new song!

new, new song, I can sing it now With the
O, the new, new song, I can sing Just now With the

ran - som'd throng: . . Pow-er and do - min-ion to him that shall
ransom'd, the ransom'd throng: . .

reign; Glo - ry and praise to the Lamb that was slain.
that shall reign;

3 Can my lips be mute, or my heart be sad,
When the gracious Master hath made me glad?
When he points where the many mansions be,
And sweetly says, 'There is one for thee'?

4 I shall catch the gleam of its jasper wall
When I come to the gloom of the evenfall,
For I know that the shadows, dreary and dim,
Have a path of light that will lead to him.

From "Gems of Praise," by per.

Fill Me Now.

Rev. E. H. Stokes, D.D.   Jno. R. Sweney.

1. Hov- er o'er me, Ho - ly Spir - it; Bathe my trembling heart and brow;
2. Thou can'st fill me, gracious Spir - it, Tho' I can - not tell thee how;
3. I am weakness, full of weakness; At thy sa - cred feet I bow;
4. Cleanse and comfort; bless and save me; Bathe, oh, bathe my heart and brow!

Fine.

Fill me with thy hal - low'd presence, Come, oh, come and fill me now.
But I need thee, great- ly need thee, Come, oh, come and fill me now.
Blest, di- vine, e - ter - nal Spir - it, Fill with power, and fill me now.
Thou art comfort - ing and sav- ing, Thou art sweet - ly fill - ing now.

D.S. Fill me with thy hal-low'd presence,—Come, oh, come and fill me now.

CHORUS.   D.S.

Fill me now, fill me now, Je - sus, come, and fill me now;

Some Sweet Day.

ARTHUR W. FRENCH.   "The hour is coming."—John v. 28.   D. B. TOWNER. By per.

Moderato.

1. We shall reach the riv-er side Some sweet day, some sweet day;
2. We shall pass in-side the gate Some sweet day, some sweet day;
3. We shall meet our loved and own Some sweet day, some sweet day;

We shall cross the storm-y tide Some sweet day, some sweet day;
Peace and plen-ty for us wait Some sweet day, some sweet day;
Gath'ring round the great white throne Some sweet day, some sweet day;

We shall press the sands of gold, While be-fore our eyes un-fold
We shall hear the wondrous strain, Glo-ry to the Lamb that's slain,
By the tree of life so fair, Joy and rap-ture ev-'rywhere,

Heav-en's splendors, yet un-told, Some sweet day, some sweet day.
Christ was dead, but lives a-gain, Some sweet day, some sweet day.
O the bliss of o-ver there! Some sweet day, some sweet day.

O Wonderful Saviour.

E. F. M.

Isa. ix. 6.

E. F. MILLER.

1. I have heard a most wonderful sto - ry, Of Je-sus the Saviour and King,
2. With the poor and the lowly he mingled, Yes, even the vil- est of men,
3. A poor woman was brought to him, helpless, To be stoned for her sins in the past;
4. See him weep at a grave in the hour When tears of anguish are shed;
5. Yes, he came to give life to the dying, To heal all the broken in heart;

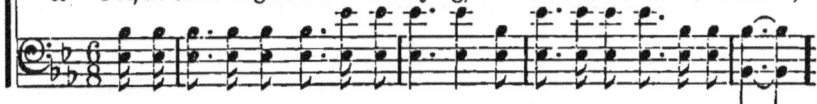

How he came from the bright realms of glory Glad news of salvation to bring.
Showing mercy and love as they lingered To hear his blest words unto them.
He re-plied to them, "He that is sinless, By him let the first stone be cast."
See him bursting the tomb by his power, Saying, "Laz'rus, come forth from the dead!
And he promised a home where's no sighing, And loved ones shall ne'er again part.

CHORUS.

O wonderful, wonderful Sav-iour, Thy praises with joy we will sing;

For coming to earth to redeem us, We crown thee forev - er our King.

By permission of E. F. Miller.

Tell it to Jesus.

J. E. RANKIN, D. D.   Matt. xiv. 12.   E. S. LORENZ.

1. Are you wea-ry, are you heavy-heart-ed? Tell it to Je-sus,
2. Do the tears flow down your cheeks unbidden? Tell it to Je-sus,
3. Do you fear the gath'ring clouds of sor-row? Tell it to Je-sus,
4. Are you trou-bled at the thought of dy-ing? Tell it to Je-sus,

Tell it to Je-sus; Are you griev-ing o-ver joys de-part-ed?
Tell it to Je-sus; Have you sins that to man's eye are hid-den?
Tell it to Je-sus; Are you anx-ious what shall be to-mor-row?
Tell it to Je-sus; For Christ's coming Kingdom are you sigh-ing?

CHORUS.

Tell it to Je-sus a-lone. Tell it to Je-sus, Tell it to Je-sus,

He is a friend that's well known; You have no oth-er

such a friend or broth-er, Tell it to Je-sus a-lone.

DO RE MI FA SO LA SI

He Saves.

Frank M. Davis.　　　　John iii 17.　　　　E. C. Avis.

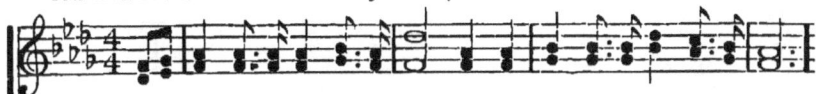

1. Sing glo - ry to God in the highest, For wonderful things he hath done;
2. Oh! perfect redemption to sinners, The purchase of Jesus' own blood,
3. Rejoice, then, rejoice, all ye peo- ple, The wondrous transaction is done!

He so loved the world that he gave us His on - ly be- gotten dear Son.
The vil- est offend - er is pardoned, Is saved thro' the promise of God.
The life-gate is o - pen, come, ent- er, Thro' Jesus, the Cru - cified One.

CHORUS.

Hal- le - lu - jah! hal-le - lu - jah! He saves thro' the death of his Son;
Hal-le-lu-jah!　　　hal - le-lu-jah!

Hal- le - lu - jah! hal-le - lu - jah! He saves thro' the Crucified One.
Hal-le-lu-jah!　　　hal-le-lu-jah!

Blessed Assurance.

F. J. CROSBY.   " He is faithful that hath promised."—Heb. x. 23.   Mrs. Jos. F. KNAPP.

1. Blessed as - surance, Jesus is mine! Oh, what a foretaste of
2. Perfect sub-mis-sion, perfect de - light, Visions of rap - ture
3. Perfect sub-mis-sion, all is at rest, I in my Saviour am

glory di - vine! Heir of sal - va - tion, purchase of God, Born of his
burst on my sight, Angels descend- ing, bring from a - bove Echoes of
happy and blest, Watching and waiting, looking a - bove, Filled with his

CHORUS.

Spir - it, washed in his blood. This is my sto - ry, this is my
mer - cy, whispers of love.
goodness, lost in his love.

song, Praising my Sav - iour all the day long; This is my

sto - ry, this is my song, Praising my Saviour all the day long.

Copyright 1873, by Joseph F. Knapp.

Is not this the Land of Beulah.

31

ANON.

ARRANGED.

1. I am dwell-ing on the mountain, Where the gold-en sunlight gleams
2. I can see far down the mountain, Where I wandered wea-ry years,
3. I am drink-ing at the fountain, Where I ev - er would a-bide;

O'er a land whose wondrous beauty Far ex-ceeds my fondest dreams;
Oft - en hin-dered in my jour-ney By the ghosts of doubts and fears,
For I've tast - ed life's pure riv - er, And my soul is sat-is-fied;

Where the air is pure, e - the-real, Laden with the breath of flowers,
Brok-en vows and dis-appointments Thickly sprinkled all the way,
There's no thirst-ing for life's pleasures, Nor a-dorn - ing, rich and gay,

CHO.—Is not this the land of Beu-lah, Blessed, bles - sed land of light,

D. S. Chorus.

They are blooming by the fountain, 'Neath the am - a-ranthine bowers.
But the Spir - it led, un - er-ring, To the land I hold to-day.
For I've found a rich-er treasure, One that fad - eth not a - way.

Where the flow-ers bloom for-ev - er, And the sun is always bright.

4 Tell me not of heavy crosses,
   Nor the burdens hard to bear,
For I've found this great salvation
Makes each burden light appear;
And I love to follow Jesus,
   Gladly counting all but dross,
Worldly honors all forsaking
For the glory of the Cross.

5 Oh, the Cross has wondrous glory!
   Oft I've proved this to be true;
When I'm in the way so narrow
   I can see a pathway through;
And how sweetly Jesus whispers:
   Take the Cross, thou need'st not fear,
For I've tried this way before thee,
   And the glory lingers near.

Is my Name written There?

M. A. K.

FRANK M. DAVIS.

1. Lord, I care not for riches, Neither silver nor gold; I would make sure of
2. Lord, my sins they are many, Like the sands of the sea, But thy blood, O my
3. Oh! that beauti - ful cit - y, With its mansions of light, With its glorified

heaven, I would en-ter the fold; In the book of thy kingdom, With its
Saviour! is suf - fi-cient for me; For thy promise is written, In bright
be-ings, In pure garments of white; Where no evil thing cometh, To de-

pag- es so fair, Tell me, Jesus, my Saviour, Is my name written there?
let- ters that glow, "Tho' your sins be as scarlet, I will make them like snow."
spoil what is fair; Where the angels are watching,—Is my name written there?

REFRAIN.

Is my name writ-ten there, On the page white and fair?

In the book of thy king-dom, Is my name written there?

DO RE MI FA SO LA SI

Is Your Lamp Burning.

"Let your light so shine before men, that they may see your good works, and glorify your Father which is in heaven."—Matt. v. 16.

Mrs. E. M. H. Gates.   C. C. Williams.

1. Say, is your lamp burning, my brother? I pray you look quickly and see;
2. Upon the dark mountains they stumble, They are bruised on the rocks as they lie
3. If once all the lamps that are lighted Should steadily blaze in a line,

For if it were burning, then surely, Some beam would fall brightly on me.
With white, pleading faces turned upward, To the clouds and the pitiful sky.
Wide o - ver the land and the o - cean, What a girdle of glory would shine!

There are many and many around you, Who follow wherever you go,
There is many a lamp that is lighted—We behold them a-near and a-far;
How all the dark places would brighten! How the mists would turn up and away!

D.S. Say, is your lamp burning, my brother? I pray you look quickly and see;

D.S. for Chorus.

If you tho't that they walked in the shadow, Your lamp would burn brighter, I know
But not many among them, my brother, Shine steadily on like a star.
How the earth would laugh out in her gladness, To hail the millennial day!

For if it were burning, then surely, Some beam would fall brightly on me!

Temple Songs-C

The New "Over There."

W. A. Ogden.

1. They have reach'd the sunny shore, And will never hunger more, All their
2. Now they feel no chilling blast, For their winter time is past, And their
3. They have fought the weary fight, Jesus sav'd them by his might, Now they

grief and pains are o'er, Over there; And they need no lamp by night, For their
summers always last, O- ver there; They can never know a fear, For the
dwell with him in light, Over there; Soon we'll reach the shining strand, But we'll

D. S.—All their streets are shining gold, And their

Fine. CHORUS.

day is always bright, And their Saviour is their light, Over there. O - ver
Saviour's always near, And with them is endless cheer, Over there.
wait our Lord's command, 'Till we see his beck'ning hand, Over there.

glo-ry is untold, 'Tis the Saviour's blissful fold, O- ver there.

D.S.

there, over there, They can never know a fear, Over there;
over there, over there, over there;

From " New Silver Song," by per.

conquer-ors, We are more than conquerors Thro' him that loved us.

More Faith in Jesus.

Henrietta E. Blair. Wm. J. Kirkpatrick.

1. While struggling thro' this vale of tears I want more faith in Je-sus; A-
2. To war against the foes with-in I want more faith in Je-sus; To
3. To brave the storms that here I meet I want more faith in Je-sus; To
4. I want a faith that works by love, A constant faith in Je-sus; A

D. S.—And

Fine. CHORUS.

mid tempta-tions, cares, and fears, I want more faith in Je - sus. I
rise a-bove the powers of sin I want more faith in Je - sus.
rest con-fid-ing at his feet I want more faith in Je - sus.
faith that mountains can remove, A liv-ing faith in Je - sus.

this my cry, as time rolls by, I want more faith in Je - sus.

D. S.

want more faith, I want more faith, A clearer, brighter, stronger faith in Jesus;

Are You Drifting?

MARY D. JAMES.

WM. J. KIRKPATRICK.

1. Are you drifting down life's current, Drift-ing on a dang'rous tide?
2. Down the stream of worldly pleasure Drift-ing, drifting ev - er- more
3. Heed, oh, heed the kind moni - tion! Give your aimless wand'rings o'er;

Near the rapids' fearful per - il All unconscious do ye glide?
T'ward the great unfathomed o - cean, Bound for yon e - ter-nal shore?
Cease to seek in earth your pleasure, Head your bark for heav'n's bright shore,

Down the stream of sin and fol - ly,—Heed-ing not the danger near,
Drift - ing, drifting,—going,—whither? Aim - less, purposeless;—how vain!
Take on board the skillful pi - lot, Use the oars of faith and prayer;

Drift - ing on in self-com-pla - cence, Feel - ing no remorse or fear?
To the dark and dread forev - er! What, oh, what have ye to gain?
Then you'll make the port of glo - ry, God will guide you safely there.

CHORUS.

Hark the voice . . of yonder pilot: Cease your drifting, seize the oar;
Hark the voice, the warning voice of yonder pilot: seize the oar;

Make the blest, celestial harbor, Steer your bark for Canaan's shore.

Make the blest, celestial harbor, make the harbor,

Light after Darkness.

JNO. R. SWENEY.

DUET.

1. Light af-ter dark-ness, Gain af-ter loss, Strength af-ter
2. Sheaves af-ter sow-ing, Sun af-ter rain, Sight af-ter
3. Near af-ter dis-tant, Gleam af-ter gloom, Love af-ter

weak-ness, Crown af-ter cross, Sweet af-ter bit-ter,
mys-tery, Peace af-ter pain, Joy af-ter sor-row,
loneliness, Life af-ter tomb; Af-ter long a-go-ny,

Song af-ter fears, Home af-ter wan-der-ing, Praise af-ter tears.
Calm af-ter blast, Rest af-ter wea-riness,—Sweet rest at last.
Rap-ture of bliss; Right was the path-way Leading to this!

From "Goodly Pearls," by per.

God so Loved the World.

FANNY J. CROSBY. John iii. 16. WM. J. KIRKPATRICK.

Solo ad lib.

1. God loved the world so tenderly His only Son he gave, That all who on his
2. Oh, love that only God can feel, And only he can show! Its height and depth, its
3. Why perish, then, ye ransom'd ones? Why slight the gracious call? Why turn from him
4. O Saviour, melt these hearts of ours, And teach us to believe That whosoever [whose

CHORUS.

name believe Its wondrous pow'r will save. For God so loved the world that he
length and breadth Nor heav'n nor earth can know!
words proclaim E-ter-nal life to all?
comes to thee Shall endless life receive.

gave his on - ly Son, That who - so - ev - er be - lieveth in him

Should not per - ish, should not per - ish; That who - so - ev - er be -

lieveth in him Should not per - ish, but have ev - er - last - ing life.

DO RE MI FA SO LA SI

Leading Souls to Jesus.

J. E. Rankin, D. D.　　　　　　　　　　　　　　　　　Jno. R. Sweney.

1. Leading souls to Jesus who are sad and lost, Who upon life's waters have been
2. Leading souls to Jesus, telling them the way Out of nature's darkness into
3. Leading souls to Jesus from their want and sin, Setting up his kingdom with its
4. Leading souls to Jesus, as the stars to shine, In some humbly station, Master,

tempest-tossed; All the heavy-laden, burdened with their load, Whisp'ring of sal-
God's own day; Kneeling with the sinner at the Saviour's feet, Even angels
peace within; Till the Spirit witness in them o'er and o'er, Cleans'd are thy trans-
be　it　mine; With forgiven sin-ners, not alone, to stand When I rise to

CHORUS.

vation thro' the Lamb of God. Leading souls to Jesus! oh, may this be mine,
can not know of work more sweet.
gressions: go, and sin no more.
glo-ry in the bet - ter land.

Till I cross the riv - er　to that home divine; Sowing by all wa - ters,

till the great day come, When with joy the reapers shout the harvest home.

DO　RE　MI　FA　SO　LA　SI

44 O Prodigal, Don't Stay Away.

J. E. RANKIN, D. D.   "I will arise and go unto my Father."—Luke xv. 18.   J. W. BISCHOFF.

1. O prod-i-gal, don't stay away! The Fa-ther is waiting to-day; There's
2. O prodigal brother, come home! Why longer in wretchedness roam? You're
3. O prodigal, what will you do? Love's ta-ble is wait-ing for you; For-
4. O prod-i-gal brother, a-rise! For pardon, look up to the skies; No

room and to spare, There is raiment to wear, O prod-igal, don't stay a-way.
lone-ly and lost, You are driven and toss'd, O prod-igal brother, come home.
giveness so sweet, Sure, your coming will greet, O prodigal, what will you do?
longer then stray From thy Father away, O prod-i-gal brother, a-rise.

CHORUS.

Will you come? Will you come? Will you come, come home to-day? There is

Will you come?   Will you come?   Will you come?

welcome for you, There's a kiss, kind and true, Then, O prodigal, don't stay away.

Marching On.

JENNIE GARNETT.   WM. J. KIRKPATRICK.

1. With our col-ors waving bright in the blaze of gos-pel light We are
2. Oft the tempter we shall meet, but we will not fear de-feat, Though his
3. We have gird-ed on the sword and the ar-mor of the Lord, We have
4. Soon we'll reach the pearly gate, where the blessed army wait, Soon their

marshall'd on the world's great field; great field; We are ready for the strife and the
arrows at our ranks may fly; may fly; Thro' a Saviour's mighty love more than
ta-ken up the cross he bore; he bore; Oh, the trophies we shall win, oh, the
welcome, welcome song may ring; may ring; When we lay our armor down and re-

bat-tle work of life, Ev-er trusting in the Lord our shield.
conquerors we shall prove, Shouting, Glo-ry be to God on high.
vic-tory o-ver sin, When the bat-tle and the strife are o'er!
ceive a star-ry crown, Shouting, Glo-ry be to God our King.

CHORUS.

Glo-ry to God! we are marching, marching on, Marching to a home above;

Glo-ry to God! we are marching, marching on, Happy in a Saviour's love.

Glory to Jesus, He Saves.

P. B.

P. Bilhorn.

1. Glo - ry to Je - sus who died on the tree, Paid the great price that my
2. Once in my heart there was sin and despair, Now the dear Saviour him-
3. Come, then, ye wea - ry, who long to be free, Come to the Saviour, he

soul might be free; Now I can sing hal - le - lu - jah to God,
self dwelleth there, And from his pres - ence comes peace to my soul,
wait - eth for thee; Then with the ransomed this song you can sing,

CHORUS.

Glo - ry! he saves, he saves. Glo - ry! he saves, glo - ry! he saves,

Saves a poor sin - ner like me; Glo - ry! he saves,

glo - ry! he saves, Saves a poor sin - ner like me. like me.

'Tis the Blessed Hour of Prayer.

47

"—— went into the temple at the hour of prayer."
Acts iii. 1

FANNY J. CROSBY.   W. H. DOANE. By per.

1. 'Tis the bless-ed hour of prayer, when our hearts lowly bend, And we
2. 'Tis the bless-ed hour of prayer, when the Saviour draws near, With a
3. 'Tis the bless-ed hour of prayer, when the tempted and tried To the
4. At the bless-ed hour of prayer, trusting him we be-lieve That the

gath-er to Je-sus, our Sav-iour and Friend; If we come to him in
ten-der com-pas-sion his chil-dren to hear; When he tells us we may
Saviour who loves them their sorrow con-fide; With a sym-pathiz-ing
blessing we're needing we'll sure-ly re-ceive, In the ful-ness of this

faith, his protec-tion to share, What a balm for the wea-ry! oh, how
cast at his feet ev-'ry care, What a balm for the wea-ry! oh, how
heart he removes ev-'ry care; What a balm for the wea-ry! oh, how
trust we shall lose ev-'ry care; What a balm for the wea-ry! oh, how

Fine. CHORUS.   D.S.

sweet to be there! Blessed hour of prayer, Blessed hour of prayer;

Copyright, 1880, by Biglow & Main.

The Promises.

L. E. Hewitt.

Jno. R. Sweney.

1. The prom - is - es, how precious! The words of God's own book! They
2. They fall up - on waste plac- es Like gen - tle drops of rain, Re-
3. Yes, they shall stand forev - er! God's word shall still endure, A-

shine amid our darkness Like stars on some lone brook; Or, like the joy-ous
fresh-ing and uplifting The soul that's faint with pain. They speak a Father's
mid time's devas-tations E - ter - nal-ly secure. He's faithful that hath

sunshine. They fill our path with light, The fore-gleams of that glory Where
blessing, They breathe a Saviour's love; Our comfort in life's sorrows, Our
promised, I trust his words divine; Oh, show me all their fulness, Blest

CHORUS.

com - eth no more night.
pledge of joys a - bove. The prom - is - es, how pre - cious! I
Spir - it, make them mine.

love to call them mine. Sealed by my Saviour's dying blood, In covenant divine.

Oh, Sing of His Mighty Love.

49

"Mighty to save."—Isa. xliii. 1.

Rev. Frank Bottome, D. D

Wm. B. Bradbury. By per.

1. Oh, bliss of the pu-ri-fied, bliss of the free, I plunge in the crimson tide
2. Oh, bliss of the pu-ri-fied, Je-sus is mine, No long-er in dread condem
3. Oh, bliss of the purified, bliss of the pure! No wound hath the soul that his
4. O Je-sus the crucified! thee will I sing, My blessed Redeemer, my

opened for me; O'er sin and uncleanness ex-ult-ing I stand, And
na-tion I pine; In conscious sal-vation I sing of his grace, Who
blood cannot cure, No sor-row bowed head but may sweetly find rest, No
God and my King; My soul, filled with rapture, shall shout o'er the grave, And

CHORUS.

point to the print of the nails in his hand. Oh, sing of his mighty love,
lift-eth up-on me the light of his face.
tears but may dry them on Jesus' breast.
triumph in death in the "Mighty to save."

rit.

Sing of his mighty love, sing of his mighty love, Mighty to save.

Copyright, 1867, 1890, used by per Biglow & Main.

Temple Songs–D

The Future.

Miss Jennie Stout.　　　　　　　　　　　　　　　　　　A. A. Armen.

1. Oh, I oft-en sit and pon-der, When the sun is sink-ing low,
2. Shall I be at work for Je-sus, Whilst he leads me by the hand,
3. But perhaps my work for Je-sus Soon in fu-ture may be done,

Where shall yonder fu-ture find me: Does but God in heav-en know?
And to those a-round be say - ing, Come and join his hap-py band?
All my earthly tri - als end - ed, And my crown in heav-en won;

Shall I be a-mong the liv - ing? Shall I min-gle with the free?
Come, for all things now are rea - dy, Come, his faithful foll-'wer be;
Then for-ev - er with the ran-somed Thro' e - ter - ni - ty I'd be

Where-so-e'er my path be lead-ing, Saviour, keep my heart with thee.
Oh, where'er my path be lead-ing, Saviour, keep my heart with thee.
Chanting hymns to him who bought me With his blood shed on the tree.

CHORUS.

Oh, the fu - - - - ture lies be - fore me, And I
Oh, the fu-ture lies be-fore me, And I know not where I'll be, Oh, the

From "Our Sabbath Home," by per.

know . . not where I'll be, But where'er - - my path be
future lies before me, And I know not where I'll be, But where'er my path be leading, Saviour,

lead - - ing, Saviour, keep . . . my heart with thee.
keep my heart with thee, But where'er my path be leading, Saviour, keep my heart with thee.

I'll Live for Him.

C. R. DUNBAR.

1. My life, my love I give to thee, Thou Lamb of God, who died for me;
2. I now believe thou dost receive, For thou hast died that I might live;
3. Oh, thou who died on Cal - va- ry, To save my soul and make me free,

CHO.—I'll live for him who died for me, How happy then my life shall be!

D.C.

Oh, may I ev - er faith-ful be, My Saviour and my God!
And now henceforth I'll trust in thee, My Saviour and my God!
I con - secrate my life to thee, My Saviour and my God!

I'll live for him who died for me, My Saviour and my God!

By permission.

At the Cross.

R. Kelso Carter.

Arr. by E. E. Nickerson.

1. O Je-sus, Lord, thy dy-ing love Hath pierced my con-trite heart;
2. A - mid the night of sin and death Thy light hath filled my soul;
3. I kiss thy feet, I clasp thy hand, I touch thy bleed-ing side;
4. My Lord, my light, my strength, my all, I count my gain but loss;

Now take my life, and let me prove How dear to me thou art.
To me thy lov - ing voice now saith, Thy faith hath made thee whole.
O let me here for - ev - er stand, Where thou wast cru-ci - fied.
For - ev - er let thy love enthrall, And keep me at the cross.

CHORUS.

At the cross, at the cross, where I first saw the light, And the

bur-den of my heart roll'd a - way, It was there by

faith I receiv'd my sight, And now I am hap - py night and day!

Follow On!

W. O. Cushing.

Robert Lowry. By per.

1. Down in the valley with my Saviour I would go, Where the flowers are
2. Down in the valley with my Saviour I would go, Where the storms are
3. Down in the valley, or up-on the mountain steep, Close beside my

blooming and the sweet wa-ters flow; Ev'rywhere he leads me I would
sweeping and the dark wa-ters flow; With his hand to lead me I will
Saviour would my soul ev-er keep; He will lead me safely, in the

fol-low, fol-low on, Walking in his footsteps till the crown be won.
nev-er, nev-er fear, Dangers cannot fright me if my Lord is near.
path that he has trod, Up to where they gather on the hills of God.

REFRAIN.

Follow! follow! I would follow Jesus! Anywhere, ev'rywhere, I would follow on!

Follow! follow! I would follow Jesus! Ev'rywhere he leads me I will follow on!

In the Shadow of His Wings.

Rev. J. B. ATCHINSON.   E. O. EXCELL.

1. In the shadow of his wings There is rest, sweet rest; There is rest from care and
2. In the shadow of his wings There is peace, sweet peace, Peace that passeth under-
3. In the shadow of his wings There is joy, glad joy, There is joy to tell the

la - bor, There is rest for friend and neighbor, In the shadow of his wings,
standing, Peace, sweet peace that knows no ending, In the shadow of his wings,
sto - ry, Joy ex - ceeding, full of glo - ry; In the shadow of his wings,

There is rest, sweet rest, In the shadow of his wings There is rest, sweet rest,
There is peace, sweet peace, In the shadow of his wings There is peace, sweet peace,
There is joy, glad joy, In the shadow of his wings, There is joy, glad joy,

CHORUS.

There is rest,   There is peace,   There is joy   In the shadow of his wings;
sweet rest,   sweet peace,   glad joy,

There is rest,   there is peace,   There is joy   In the shadow of his wings.
sweet rest,   sweet peace,   glad joy,

Drinking at the Living Fountain.

The "Lanan."   P. Bilhorn.

1. I have found a balm for all my woe,   Jesus is the living fountain;
2. When I came to Je-sus in my sin,   Bending at the living fountain;
3. As I heard his voice so kind and sweet, Sounding at the living fountain;
4. To the fountain come, O come to-day,   Flowing is the living fountain;

I am full of   joy, as Christ I know, Drinking at the fount of   life.
Then he heard my prayer and made me clean, Cleansed me at the fount of life.
Then I wept and sang low at   his feet, Drinking at the fount of   life.
If you come he'll wash your sins a - way,   Je-sus is the fount of life.

CHORUS.

O the fount is Christ, in him believe, Drinking at the living   fountain;

All who come to him, the   life received,   Jesus   is the fount of   life.

Coming To=day.

Fanny J. Crosby.

Jno. R. Sweney.

1. Out on the des-ert, looking, looking, Sinner, 'tis Je-sus looking for thee;
2. Still he is waiting, waiting, waiting, O, what compassion beams in his eye,
3. Lovingly pleading, pleading, pleading, Mercy, tho' slighted, bears with thee yet;
4. Spirits in glory, watching, watching, Long to behold thee safe in the fold;

Tender - ly calling, calling, calling, Hither, thou lost one, O, come unto me.
Hear him repeat-ing gent-ly, gently, Come to thy Saviour, O, why wilt thou die.
Thou canst be happy, hap-py, hap-py, Come, ere thy life-star forever shall set.
Angels are waiting, waiting, waiting, When shall thy story with rapture be told?

CHORUS.

Jesus is looking, Jesus is calling, Why dost thou linger, why tarry away?

Run to him quickly, say to him gladly, Lord, I am coming, coming to-day.

The Child of a King.

HATTIE E. BUELL. Arr. from Melody by Rev. JOHN B. SUMNER.

1. My Fa-ther is rich in houses and lands, He holdeth the wealth of the
2. My Father's own Son, the Saviour of men, Once wander'd o'er earth as the
3. I once was an out-cast stranger on earth, A sin-ner by choice, an
4. A tent or a cot-tage, why should I care? They're building a palace for

world in his hands! Of ru-bies and diamonds, of silver and gold His
poorest of men, But now he is reigning for-ev-er on high, And will
al-ien by birth! But I've been a-dopt-ed, my name's written down,—An
me o-ver there! Tho' exiled from home, yet, still I may sing: All

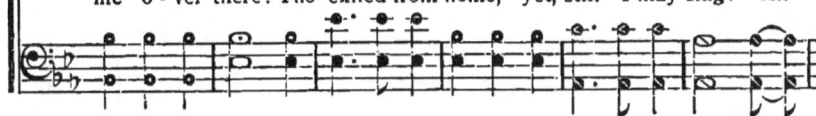

CHORUS.

cof-fers are full,—he has riches un-told. I'm the child of a King, The
give me a home in heaven by and by.
heir to a man-sion, a robe, and a crown.
glo-ry to God, I'm the child of a King.

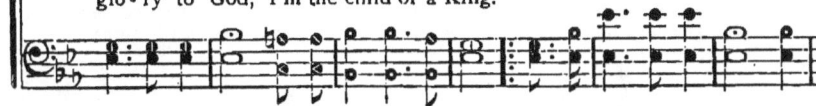

ad lib.

child of a King; With Je-sus my Saviour I'm the child of a King.

DO RE MI FA SO LA SI

By the Grace of God we'll Meet.

FANNY J. CROSBY.　　　　　　　　　　　　　　　　　　JNO. R. SWENEY.

1. Thro' the gates of pearl and jasper To the ci-ty paved with gold,When the
2. When the harvest work is ended, And the summer days are past, When the
3. Let us fol-low on with firmness, keeping ev-er in the way Where our

ransomed host shall en-ter, And their gracious Lord be-hold. When they
reap-ers go re-joic-ing To their bright re-ward at last; When the
bles-sed Lord has taught us, To be faith-ful, watch and pray; Then, in

meet in bliss-ful triumph By the tree of life so fair Shall we
white-robed an-gel leads them to the gates of joy so fair, Shall we
garments pure and spotless, By the tree of life so fair, We shall

join the no-ble arm-y, And re-ceive a wel-come there?
join their hap-py num-ber? Will they bid us wel-come there?
sing through endless ag-es With the count-less mil-lions there.

CHORUS.

By the grace . . . . . of God we'll meet . . . . . In the
By the grace of God we'll meet, By the grace of God we'll meet In the

DO RE MI FA SO LA SI

ci - ty's golden street, Shouting, glo - - - - ry! hal-le-
ci - ty's gold - en street, golden street, Shouting, glo-ry! hal-le-lu-jah! Shouting,

lu - - - - jah! At the dear - - - - - Redeem-er's feet.
glo - ry! hal-le-lu-jah! At our dear Re-deem-er's feet, Re-deem-er's feet.

A Sinner like Me.

C. J. B. CHAS. J. BUTLER.

1. I was once far away from the Saviour, And as vile as a sinner could be,

I wondered if Christ the Redeemer, Could save a poor sinner like me.

2 I wandered on in the darkness,
Not a ray of light could I see, [ness,
And the thought filled my heart with sad-
There's no hope for a sinner like me.

3 I then fully trusted in Jesus,
And oh, what a joy came to me;
My heart was filled with his praises,
For saving a sinner like me.

4 No longer in darkness I'm walking,
For the light is now shining on me,
And now unto others I'm telling,
How he saved a poor sinner like me.

5 And when life's journey is over,
And I the dear Saviour shall see,
I'll praise him forever and ever,
For saving a sinner like me.

DO RE MI FA SO LA SI

Happy Tidings.

LIZZIE EDWARDS.

JNO. R. SWENEY.

1. Tidings, happy tidings, Hark! hark! the sound! Hear the joyful e - cho
2. Tidings, happy tidings, Hark! hark! they say, Do not slight the warning,
3. Tidings, happy tidings, Hark! hark! a - gain! Rushing o'er the mountain,

Thro' the world resound; Christ the Lord proclaims them, Hear and heed the call,
Come, oh, come to-day; Christ, our lov- ing Sav- iour, Still repeats the call,
Sweeping o'er the plain; Onward goes the message, 'Tis the Saviour's call,

REFRAIN.

Come, ye starving ones that perish, Room, room for all. Whoso- ev - er ask- eth,
Come, ye weary, hea- vy- laden, Room, room for all.
Come, for ev'rything is ready, Room, room for all.

Jesus will receive; Whosoever thirsteth, Jesus will relieve; See the living

waters, Flowing full and free; Oh, the blessed whosoever! That means me.

DO RE MI FA SO LA

Jesus of Nazareth Passeth By.

Miss Etta Campbell.   Mark x. 47.   Theo. E. Perkins. By per.

1. What means this eager, anxious throng, Which moves with busy haste along—
2. Who is this Jesus? Why should he The ci - ty move so might-i - ly?
3. Je-sus! 'tis he who once be-low Man's pathway trod, 'mid pain and woe;
4. Again he comes! From place to place His ho - ly footprints we can trace.

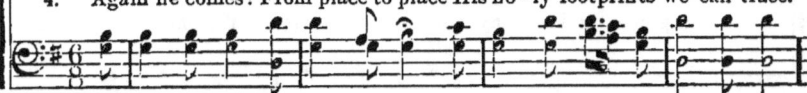

These wondrous gath'rings day by day? What means this strange commotion pray?
A pass-ing stranger, has he skill To move the mul - ti-tude at will?
And burdened ones, where'er he came, Brought out their sick, and deaf, and lame.
He paus-eth at our threshhold—nay, He en - ters—con - descends to stay.

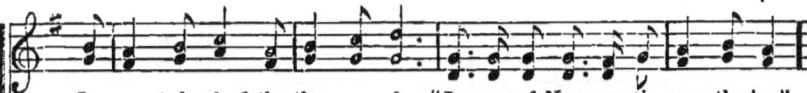

In accents hushed the throng reply: "Je-sus of Naz - areth passeth by,"
A-gain the stirring notes re-ply: "Je-sus of Naz - areth passeth by,"
The blind rejoiced to hear the cry: "Je-sus of Naz - areth passeth by,"
Shall we not glad - ly raise the cry—"Je-sus of Naz - areth passeth by,"

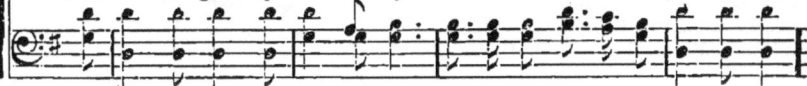

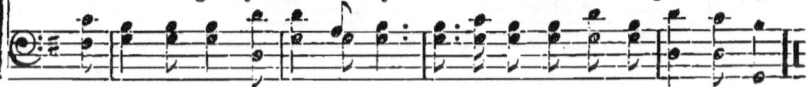

In accents hushed the throng reply: "Je-sus of Naz - areth pass-eth by."
A-gain the stirring notes re-ply: "Je-sus of Naz - areth pass-eth by."
The blind rejoiced to hear the cry: "Je-sus of Naz - areth pass-eth by."
Shall we not gladly raise the cry—"Je-sus of Naz - areth pass-eth by."

5 Ho! all ye heavy-laden, come!
  Here's pardon, comfort, rest, and home.
  Ye wanderers from a Father's face,
  Return, accept his proffered grace.
  Ye tempted ones, there's refuge nigh:
  "Jesus of Nazareth passeth by."

6 But if you still this call refuse,
  And all his wondrous love abuse,
  Soon will he sadly from you turn,
  Your bitter prayer for pardon spurn.
  "Too late! too late!" will be the cry—
  "Jesus of Nazareth *has passed by.*"

62 # The Saviour is My All in All.

P. B.   "Wherefore he is able to save them to the uttermost."—Heb. vii. 25.   P. Bilhorn.

1. The Saviour is my all in all, He is my constant theme!
2. His Spir-it gives sweet peace within, And bids all care de - part!
3. And whatso - ev - er I may ask, To glo - ri - fy his name,
4. Oh, praise the Lord, my soul, rejoice, Give thanks unto thy God!

By sim - ply trusting in his word He keeps me pure and clean.
He fills my soul with righteousness, And pu - ri - fies the heart.
The Fa - ther free - ly gives to me, Since Christ the Saviour came.
Who took thee in thy sin - fulness, And cleansed thee by his blood!

CHORUS.

Glo - ry! oh, glo - ry! Je - sus hath redeemed me;

Glo - ry! oh, glo - ry! He washed my sins a - way, a - way!

Copyright, 1888, by P. Bilhorn.

What's the News.

Words arranged by W. H. G.

Rev. W. H. GEISTWEIT.

1. Whene'er we meet we always say, "What's the news? Pray what's the
2. God has pardoned all my sin, That's the news! I feel the
3. And now if a - ny one should say, What's the news? O tell him
4. Wea - ry pilgrim, hear the call, Bless - ed news! Christ Je- sus

or - der of the day, What's the news?" His work's re - viv - ing
wit - ness deep with-in, That's the news! And since he took my
you've be - gun to pray, That's the news! That you have joined the
came to save us all, That's the news! He died to set poor

all a - round, And sin - ners hear the gos - pel sound, Re-
sins a - way, And taught me how to watch and pray, I'm
conqu'ring band, And now with joy at God's command, You're
sin - ners free, That we from death might ran - somed be, And

joic-ing in a Saviour found, That's the news! That's the news!
hap-py now from day to day, That's the news! That's the news!
marching to the bet - ter land, That's the news! That's the news!
with him reign e - ter - nal - ly, That's the news! That's the news!

God be with You.

J. E. RANKIN, D. D.

"The grace of our Lord Jesus Christ be with you."
Rom. xvi. 20.

W. G. TOMER.

1. God be with you till we meet again, By his counsels guide, uphold you,
2. God be with you till we meet again, 'Neath his wings securely hide you;
3. God be with you till we meet again, When life's perils thick confound you;
4. God be with you till we meet again, Keep love's banner floating o'er you;

With his sheep securely fold you, God be with you till we meet again.
Dai-ly manna still provide you, God be with you till we meet again.
Put his arms unfailing round you, God be with you till we meet again.
Smite death's threat'ning wave before you, God be with you till we meet again.

CHORUS.

Till we meet, till we meet, Till we meet at Je-sus' feet;

Till we meet, till we meet, till we meet, till we meet;

Till we meet, till we meet, God be with you till we meet again.

Till we meet, till we meet, till we meet,

Oh, Bless Me, Saviour.

Peter Stryker, D. D.   Wm. H. Geistweit.

1. Oh, bless me, Saviour, bless me! I come to thee for grace; Life's
2. Oh, bless me, Saviour, bless me! I come to thee for rest; My
3. Oh, bless me, Saviour, bless me! I come to thee for joy; Not

bat - tle fiercely ra- ges, Help me my foes to chase. Like Gideon's band of
wea- ry head I'd pil- low Up- on thy lov- ing breast. By day, by night I'll
on - ly peace, but gladness, and bliss without alloy.   I may not have this

he - roes, My onward way shall tend; And faint, yet still pursu - ing, I'll
trust thee, Awake, or when I sleep; Assured that thou wilt ev- er Thy
bless - ing In all its ful- ness here; 'Tis kept for me in heav - en, Where

CHORUS.

triumph in the end. Bless me now, Bless me now, Pre- cious Re-
vig - il o'er me keep. *Faster.*
nev- er falls a tear.

rit.   *Repeat pp*

deem- er, Come and bless me now.

4 Bless me, I know thou'lt bless me
  In all my pilgrim way,
And bring me where the shadows
  Will never gloom the day.
My joy is now to journey
  Close to thy loving side,
And hope with thee in glory
  Forever to abide.

Copyright, 1888, by John J. Hood   *Temple Songs-*E

The Lily of the Valley.

English Melody, arranged

1. I have found a friend in Jesus, he's ev'rything to me, He's the fairest of ten
2. He all my griefs has taken, and all my sorrows borne; In temptation he's my
3. He will never, never leave me, nor yet forsake me here, While I live by faith and

thousand to my soul; The Li-ly of the Valley, in him alone I see All I
strong and mighty tower; I have all for him forsaken, and all my idols torn From my
do his blessed will; A wall of fire about me, I've nothing now to fear; With his

D. S.—Lily of the Valley, the bright and Morning Star, He's the

Fine.

need to cleanse and make me fully whole; In sorrow he's my comfort, in
heart, and now he keeps me by his power; Tho' all the world forsake me, and
manna he my hungry soul shall fill; Then sweeping up to glo-ry to

fair-est of ten thousand to my soul. CHO.—In sorrow, etc. (*after each verse.*)

D. S.

trouble he's my stay, He tells me ev'ry care on him to roll. He's the
Satan tempts me sore, Thro' Jesus I shall safely reach the goal. He's the
see his blessed face, Where rivers of delight shall ever roll. He's the

Rise Up and Hasten.67

"Rise up, my love, my fair one, and come away."

J. DENHAM SMITH. Arr. Song of Sol. ii. 10. Arr. by JAMES McGRANAHAN.

1. Rise up, and hast-en! my soul, haste along! And speed on thy
2. Why should we linger when heaven lies before! While earth's fast re-
3. Loved ones in Je-sus they've passed on before, Now rest-ing in
4. No condem-nation! how blessed is the word, And no sep-a-

jour-ney with hope and with song; Home, home is near-ing, 'tis
ced-ing, and soon will be no more; Pleasures and treasures which
glo-ry, they weary are no more; Toils all are end-ed, and
ra-tion! for-ev-er with the Lord; He will be with us who

coming in-to view, A little more of toiling and then to earth adieu.
once here we knew, No more can they charm us with such a goal in view.
nothing now but joy, And prais-es ascending, their ev-er glad employ.
loved us long before, And Je-sus, our Je-sus, is ours for ev-er-more.

CHORUS.

1st.

Come then, come, and raise the joyful song! Ye children of the wilderness, our
Home, home, home, oh, why should we delay? The

2d.

time cannot be long. morn of heaven is dawning, we're near the break of day.

Copyright, 1881, by JAMES McGRANAHAN.

68 What a Gath'ring that will be.

J. H. K.   "Gather my saints together unto me."—Ps. l. 5.   J. H. KURZENKNABE.

1. At the sounding of the trumpet, when the saints are gather'd home, We will
2. When the angel of the Lord proclaims that time shall be no more, We shall
3. At the great and final judgement, when the hidden comes to light, When the
4. When the golden harps are sounding, and the angel bands proclaim, In tri-

greet each other by the crystal sea, With the friends and all the lov'd ones there a-
gather, and the saved and ransom'd see,   Then to meet again to-gether, on the
Lord in all his glo-ry we shall see;   At the bidding of our Saviour, "Come, ye
umphant strains the glorious jubilee;   Then to meet and join to sing the song of

crystal sea;

wait-ing us to come, What a gath'ring of the faith-ful that will be!
bright ce-lestial shore, What a gath'ring of the faith-ful that will be!
bless-ed, to my right, What a gath'ring of the faith-ful that will be!
Mos-es and the Lamb, What a gath'ring of the faith-ful that will be!

CHORUS.

What a gath - - 'ring, gath - - 'ring, At the
What a gath'ring of the loved ones when we'll meet with one an-oth - er,

sounding of the glorious ju-bi - lee! What a gath - - 'ring,
ju-bi-lee! What a gath'ring when the friends and all the

DO RE MI FA SO LA SI

gath - - - 'ring, What a gath'ring of the faith-ful that will be!
dear ones meet each oth - er,

Oh! 'tis Glory in My Soul.

FLORA L. BEST.   JNO. R. SWENEY.

1. To thy cross, dear Christ I'm clinging, All my re - fuge and my plea;
2. Long my heart hath heard thee calling, But I thrust a- side thy grace;
3. Love e - ter - nal, light e - ter- nal, Close me safe - ly, sweetly in;

Matchless is thy lov-ing kindness, Else it had not stoop'd to me.
Yet, O boundless con - de - scension, Love is shin - ing from thy face.
Sav- iour, let thy balm of healing, Ev - er keep me free from sin.

CHORUS.

Oh, 'tis glo - ry! oh, 'tis glo - ry! Oh, 'tis glo - ry in my soul,

For I've touch'd the hem of his garment, And his pow'r doth make me whole.

By permission.

DO RE MI FA SO LA SI

Calvary.

"The place which is called Calvary, there they crucified him."

Rev. W. M'K. Darwood.   Luke xxiii. 33.   Jno. R. Sweney.

1. On Calv'ry's brow   my Saviour died,   'Twas there my
2. 'Mid rending rocks   and dark'ning skies,   My Saviour
3. O Je-sus, Lord,   how can it be,   That thou shouldst

Lord   was cruci - fied: 'Twas on the cross   he bled for
bows   his head and dies;   The opening vail   reveals the
give   thy life for me,   To bear the cross   and ag-o-

me,   And purchased there   my par-don free.
way   To heaven's joys   and endless day.
ny,—   In that dread hour   on Cal - va - ry!—

mf CHORUS.   *p*   *m*   *p*   *pp*

O Cal-va - ry! dark Calva - ry! Where Jesus shed his blood for me, for me;

mf   *ff*   *mf*   *rit. p*

O Cal - va - ry! blest Cal - va - ry! 'Twas there my Saviour died for me.

Over Jordan.

Mrs. M. B. C. SLADE.   Deut. xi. 31; viii 7, 8.   J. R. MURRAY.

1. With his dear and loving care Will the Saviour lead us on, To the
2. Through the rocky wilderness Will the Saviour lead us on, To the
3. With his strong and mighty hand Will the Saviour lead us on, To that
4. In the Promised Land to be Will the Saviour lead us on, Till fair

hills and valleys fair, O - ver Jor - dan? Yes, we'll rest our weary feet
land we shall possess, O - ver Jor - dan? Yes, by night the wondrous ray,
good and pleasant land, O - ver Jor - dan? Yes, where vine and olive grow,
Canaan's shore we see, O - ver Jor - dan? Yes, to dwell with thee at last,

By the crystal waters sweet, When the peaceful shore we greet, O - ver
Cloudy pil - lar by the day, They shall guide us on our way, O - ver
And the brooks and fountains flow, Thirst nor hunger shall we know. O - ver
Guide and lead us, as thou hast, Till the parted wave be passed, O - ver

CHORUS.   1st.

Jor - dan.   O - ver Jor - dan! o - ver Jordan! Yes, we'll rest our weary feet

2d.

By the crystal waters sweet, When the peaceful shore we'll greet, Over Jordan.

From " Pure Diamonds," by per. Brainard & Sons.

Wilt thou be made whole?

W. J. K.

Wm J. Kirkpatrick.

1. Hear the foot-steps of Je- sus, He is now passing by, Bearing balm for the
2. 'Tis the voice of that Saviour, Whose mer-ci - ful call Freely off- ers sal-
3. Are you halting and struggling, O'erpowered by your sin, While the waters are
4. Bless- ed Saviour, as- sist us To rest on thy word; Let the soul-healing

wounded, Healing all who ap - ply; As he spake to the suff'rer Who
va - tion To one and to all; He is now beck'ning to him Each
troubled Can you not en - ter in? Lo, the Saviour stands waiting To
pow - er On us now be out-poured; Wash away ev- 'ry sin- spot, Take

lay at the pool, He is say-ing this moment, "Wilt thou be made whole?"
sin tainted soul, And lov- ing - ly asking, "Wilt thou be made whole?"
strengthen your soul, He is earnest-ly pleading, "Wilt thou be made whole?"
per-fect con - trol, Say to each trusting spirit, "Thy faith makes thee whole."

REFRAIN.

Wilt thou be made whole? Wilt thou be made whole? O come, wea-ry

suff'rer, O come, sin-sick soul; See, the life-stream is flow- ing, See, the

DO RE MI FA SO LA SI

cleansing waves roll, Step in - to the cur-rent and thou shalt be whole.

Glorious Fountain.

COWPER.   T. C. O'KANE.

1. { There is a fountain filled with blood, filled with blood, filled with blood, There
     And sinners plung'd beneath that flood, beneath that flood, beneath that flood, And

2. { The dy-ing thief rejoiced to see, rejoiced to see, rejoiced to see, The
     And there may I, tho' vile as he, tho' vile as he, tho' vile as he, And

is   a fount-ain filled with bood, Drawn from Imman- uel's veins,
sinners plunged beneath that flood, Lose all their guilt - y stains.
dy - ing thief rejoiced to see That fount-ain in his day,
there may I, tho' vile as he, Wash all my sins a - way.

CHORUS.

Oh, glo - ri - ous fount-ain! Here will I stay, And in thee

ev - er Wash my sins a - way.

3 Thou dying Lamb, ||: thy precious blood :||
Shall never lose its power,
Till all the ransomed ||:Church of God :||
Are saved, to sin no more.

4 E'er since by faith ||: I saw the stream :||
Thy flowing wounds supply,
Redeeming love ||: has been my theme,:||
And shall be till I die.

DO RE MI FA SO LA SI

74   Nothing but the Blood of Jesus.

R. Lowry.   R. Lowry.

1. What can wash a - way my stain? Nothing but the blood of Je - sus;
2. For my cleansing this I see— Nothing but the blood of Je - sus;
3. Noth-ing can for sin a - tone— Nothing but the blood of Je - sus;
4. This is all my hope and peace— Nothing but the blood of Je - sus;

What can make me whole a - gain? Nothing but the blood of Je - sus.
For my par-don this my plea— Nothing but the blood of Je - sus.
Naught of good that I have done— Nothing but the blood of Je - sus.
This is all my righteous-ness— Nothing but the blood of Je - sus.

REFRAIN.

Oh, pre-cious is the flow That makes me white as snow;

No oth - er fount I know, Nothing but the blood of Je - sus.

5 Now by this I'll overcome—
   Nothing but the blood of Jesus;
  Now by this I'll reach my home —
   Nothing but the blood of Jesus.

6 Glory! glory! thus I sing—
   Nothing but the blood of Jesus;
  All my praise for this I bring—
   Nothing but the blood of Jesus.

Memories of Galilee.

Robert Morris, LL. D.   "Jesus walked in Galilee."—John vii. 1.   H. R. Palmer.

1. Each coo- ing dove   and sighing bough,   That makes the
2. Each flowery glen   and mossy dell,   Where hap- py
3. And when I read   the thrilling lore   Of him who

eve   so blest to me,   Has something far   divin - er
birds   in song a - gree,   Thro' sunny morn   the praises
walked   up- on the sea,   I long, oh, how   I long once

now,   It bears me back   to Gal - i - lee.
tell   Of sights and sounds   in Gal - i - lee.
more   To follow him   in Gal - i - lee.

CHORUS.

O Gal - i - lee! sweet Gal- i - lee! Where Jesus loved so much to be; O

Gal - i - lee! blue Gal - i - lee! Come, sing thy song again to me!

By permission.

DO   RE   MI   FA   SO   LA   SI

Until Ye Find.

Rev. E. H. Stokes, D. D.

Luke xv.

Jno. R. Sweney.

Andante con espress.

1. A - las! a - las! a wayward sheep Had wandered from the fold, Par
2. He sought with many-a footstep sore, From early morn till night; Thro'
3. How long, O Lord, must I still go? How long search for the sheep? They've

o'er the mountains rough and steep, Where howling tempests rolled; The
rock - y wastes, where torrents roar, —All pathways but the right; Then
wandered far a - way, I know,—Discouraged, lo, I weep: How

Shepherd, with a burdened mind, Went forth the missing one to find, The
cried, with sad and burdened mind, The missing I have failed to find, The
long thus go, with burdened mind? "Go," Jesus saith, "until ye find;" The

miss - ing one, far, far a - way, The miss - ing one to find.
miss - ing one, far, far a - way, A - las! I've failed to find.
miss - ing one must not be lost,— Go, seek un - til ye find!

CHORUS.

Go, seek un - til ye find; Go, seek un - til ye find; The
Chorus to last verse:—
Joy! joy! the lost is found; Joy! joy! the lost is found; The

miss - ing one must not be lost,—Go, seek un - til ye find.
miss - ing one, no long - er lost, The miss-ing one is found.

4 I've sought my friends for many-a day,
  Have prayed for many-a year;
Yet, still they wander far away,
  O'er mountains dark and drear;
How long thus seek with burdened mind?
"Seek," Jesus saith, "until ye find;"
  The missing one must not be lost,—
  "Go, seek until ye find!"

5 Lord, at thy word I go again,
  Believing I shall find:
I listened, and a low refrain
  Came to me on the wind;
Led by the sadly joyful sound
I rushed, and, lo, the lost was found!
  Joy! joy! O blessed joy divine!
  The lost one I have found.

Trustingly.

H. Bonar.   Wm. J. Kirkpatrick.

1. Trust - ing - ly, trust - ing - ly, Je - sus, to thee Come I; Lord,
2. Peace - ful - ly, peace - ful - ly Walk I with thee; Je - sus, my
3. Hap - pi - ly, hap - pi - ly Pass I a - long, Ea - ger to

lov - ing - ly, Come thou to me! Then shall I lov - ing - ly,
Lord, thou art All, all to me; Peace thou hast left to us,
work for thee, Ear-nest and strong; Life is for ser - vice true,

rit.

Then shall I joy - ful - ly walk here with thee, Walk here with thee.
Thy peace hast giv-en us; So let it be, So let it be.
Life is for bat-tle, too, Life is for song, Life is for song.

78 Praise and Magnify our King.

LIZZIE EDWARDS. JNO. R. SWENEY.

1. Great is the Lord, who rul-eth o-ver all! Wake, wake and sing,
2. Great is the Lord, who spake and it was done; Wake, wake and sing,
3. Great is the Lord, oh, come with ho-ly mirth; Wake, wake and sing,
4. Great is the Lord, and ho-ly is his name! Wake, wake and sing,

wake, wake and sing; Down at his feet in ad-o-ra-tion fall,
wake, wake and sing; Hon-or and strength, dominion he has won,
wake, wake and sing, Come and re-joice, ye na-tions of the earth,
wake, wake and sing; An-gels and men, his wondrous works proclaim,

CHORUS.

Praise and mag-ni-fy our King. O ye redeemed above, Strike, strike your

harps of love, Hail the Blessed One, Hail the Mighty One, Sweetly his

wonders tell, Loud-ly his glo-ry swell, Praise and magni-fy our King.

Take me as I am.

ANON.　　　　　　　　　　　　　　　　Rev. J. H. STOCKTON.

1. Je-sus, my Lord, to thee I cry, Unless thou help me I must die;
2. Helpless I am, and full of guilt, But yet for me thy blood was spilt,
3. I thirst, I long to know thy love, Thy full sal-vation I would prove;
4. If thou hast work for me to do, Inspire my will, my heart renew,
5. And when at last the work is done, The bat-tle o'er, the vic-t'ry won,

Oh, bring thy free sal - va- tion nigh, And take me as I am!
And thou can'st make me what thou wilt, But take me as I am!
But since to thee I can-not move, Oh, take me as I am!
And work both in and by me, too, But take me as I am!
Still, still my cry shall be a-lone, Oh, take me as I am!

D. S.— bring thy free sal - va- tion nigh, And take me as I am!

REFRAIN.　　　　　　　　　　　　　　　　D. S.

Take me as I am, Take me as I am; Oh,
Take me, take me as I am, Take me, take me as I am:

DO RE MI FA SO LA SI

CHARLOTTE ELLIOTT.　　　**JUST AS I AM.**　　　Tune and Chorus above.

1 JUST as I am, without one plea,
But that thy blood was shed for me,
And that thou bid'st me come to thee,
O Lamb of God, I come!

2 Just as I am, and waiting not
To rid my soul of one dark blot,
To thee whose blood can cleanse each
O Lamb of God, I come! [spot,

3 Just as I am, though tossed about
With many a conflict, many a doubt,
Fightings within, and fears without,
O Lamb of God, I come!

4 Just as I am—poor, wretched, blind;
Sight, riches, healing of the mind,
Yea, all I need, in thee to find,
O Lamb of God, I come!

5 Just as I am—thou wilt receive,
Wilt welcome, pardon, cleanse, relieve;
Because thy promise I believe,
O Lamb of God, I come!

6 Just as I am—thy love unknown
Hath broken every barrier down,
Now, to be thine, yea, thine alone,
O Lamb of God, I come!

Hiding in Thee.

"My strong rock, for a house of defense."
Ps. xxxi. 2.

Rev. William O. Cushing   Ira. D. Sankey. By per.

1. O safe to the Rock that is high-er than I, My soul in its
2. In the calm of the noontide, in sorrow's lone hour, In times when temp-
3. How oft in the conflict, when pressed by the foe, I have fled to my

conflicts and sor-rows would fly; So sin - ful, so wea - ry, thine,
ta - tion casts o'er me its power; In the tempests of life, on its
Re - fuge and breathed out my woe; How oft - en, when tri - als like

thine would I be; Thou blest "Rock of A - ges," I'm hid-ing in thee.
wide, heaving sea, Thou blest "Rock of A - ges," I'm hid-ing in thee.
sea - billows roll, Have I hid - den in thee, O thou Rock of my soul.

REFRAIN.

Hiding in thee, Hiding in thee, Thou blest "Rock of Ages," I'm hiding in thee.

Bearing my burden of woe, . . . Loving and suf-fering so.
Bear - - - ing my bur-den of woe, suf-fering so.
Who, upon Calva-ry's tree, . . . Purchased salvation for me. . . .
Who, ... up-on Cal-va-ry's tree, sal - vation for me.
This the dear wish of my soul, . . Now to be perfect-ly whole. . .
This . . . . the dear wish of my soul, perfect-ly whole.

Whosoever.

JAMES NICHOLSON.   JNO. R. SWENEY.

1. I praise the Lord that one like me For mercy may to Je-sus flee,
2. I was to sin a wretched slave, But Jesus died my soul to save;
3. I look by faith and see this word, Stamp'd with the blood of Christ my Lord,
4. I now believe he saves my soul, His precious blood hath made me whole;

He says that whoso - ev - er will May seek and find salva - tion still.
He says that whoso - ev - er will May seek and find salva - tion still.
He says that whoso - ev - er will May seek and find salva - tion still.
He says that whoso - ev - er will May seek and find salva - tion still.

CHORUS.

My Saviour's promise faileth never; He counts ME in the Whoso-ev-er.

By permission.

Christ Arose!

R. L. By per.   "He is not here, but is risen."—Luke xxiv. 6.   Rev. Robert Lowry.

Slow.

1. Low in the grave he lay—Je-sus, my Sav-iour! Waiting the coming day—
2. Vainly they watch his bed—Jesus, my Sav-iour! Vainly they seal the dead—
3. Death cannot keep his prey—Jesus, my Sav-iour! He tore the bars away—

CHORUS. *faster.*

Je - sus, my Lord! Up from the grave he a-rose, he a-rose, With a

might-y triumph o'er his foes; he a-rose! He a-rose a Victor from the

dark do-main, And he lives for - ev - er with his saints to reign: He a-

rit.

rose! he a - rose! Hal - le - lu - jah! Christ a - rose!

He a-rose! he a-rose!

DO RE MI FA SOL LA SI

Walk in the Light.

99

Asa Hull. Isaiah ii. 5. Geo. C. Hugg.

1. Walk in the light the Lord hath given, To guide thy steps a - right; His
2. Walk in the light of gospel truth, That shines from God's own word; A
3. Walk in the light! tho' shadows dark, Like spectres cross thy way; Dark-
4. Walk in the light! and thou shalt know The love of God to thee; The

CHORUS.

Holy Spirit sent from heaven, Can cheer the darkest night. Walk in the
light to guide in early youth The faithful of the Lord.
ness will flee before the light Of God's e - ter - nal day.
fellowship, so sweet below, In heaven will sweeter be. Walk in the light, in the

light, ... walk ... in the light, ...
beauti - ful light of God, Walk in the light, in the beauti - ful light of God,

Walk .. in the light, ... Walk in the light, the light of God.
Walk in the light, in the beautiful light of God;

Copyright, 1876, by Asa Hull.

The Healing Touch.

"When she heard of Jesus, came in the press behind, and touched his garment."
Mark v. 27.

Mrs. E. C. Ellsworth.

Wm. J. Kirkpatrick.

1. An ea - ger, restless crowd drew near, And round the Saviour pressed;
2. The mul - ti - tude, with curious eyes, Just gazed up - on his face;
3. Oh, near to Christ the man - y came, In that most fa - vored hour!
4. Of all who throng his courts to-day Who shall re - ceive his word?

But one, with warm and lov - ing faith, His heal - ing power confessed.
But she glanced up with hope and love, To feel his sav - ing grace.
But one stretched out the hand of faith, And touched his healing power.
Who shall reach forth with faith sincere To touch the heal - ing Lord?

CHORUS.

She had touched the hem of his garment, Trusting with all her soul;
last v. Come and touch the hem of his garment, Trusting with all your soul;

For ev - 'ry touch of the lov - ing Je - sus Can make the wounded whole.

Come to the Arms of Jesus.

Rev. M. L. Hofford. "To-day if ye will hear his voice."—Ps. xcv. 7. T. M. Miller.

1. Come to the arms of Je - sus, O come without de - lay,
2. Come to the arms of Je - sus, Re - cline on his dear breast,
3. Come to the arms of Je - sus, And when the shades of night

Come while the voice of mer - cy Is call - ing you to - day.
Come, for the heav - y la - den Can find no sweet- er rest.
Have wrapped the world in darkness, In him you shall have light.

DUET.

The gold - en gates are o - pen, To your celes - tial home,
His lov - ing voice is call - ing, En - treat - ing you to come,
Come while the Spir - it bids you, In sweet - est tones to come;

CHORUS.

The shin - ing ones are wait - ing To hear you say, "I come."
His gen - tle arms are wait - ing To give you welcome home,
The gold - en gates are o - pen To your ce - les - tial home,

The shin - ing ones are wait - ing, To hear you say, "I come."
His gen - tle arms are wait - ing To give you wel - come home.
The gold - en gates are o - pen To your ce - les - tial home.

By permission of E. T. Gordon & Son.

It Reaches Me.

MARY D. JAMES.   JNO. R. SWENEY.

1. Oh, this ut - ter - most sal - va - tion! 'Tis a fountain full and free,
2. How a - maz - ing God's compassion, That so vile a worm should prove
3. Je - sus, Saviour, I a - dore thee! Now thy love I will proclaim,

Pure, ex - haustless, ev - er flow - ing, Wondrous grace! it reaches me!
This stupend - ous bliss of Heav - en, This un - measured wealth of love!
I will tell the blessed sto - ry, I will mag - ni - fy thy name!

CHORUS.

It reaches me! it reaches me! Wondrous grace! it reaches me!

Pure, ex - haustless, ev - er flowing, Wondrous grace! it reaches me!

From "The Garner," by per.

DO RE MI FA SO LA SI

T. C. O'KANE.   By per.

1. On Jor-dan's storm-y banks I stand, And cast a wish-ful eye
2. O'er all these wide-ex-tend-ed plains Shines one e-ter-nal day;
3. When shall I reach that hap-py place, And be for-ev-er blest?
4. Filled with delight, my rap-tured soul Would here no long-er stay;

To Canaan's fair and hap-py land, Where my pos-ses-sions lie.
There God the Son for-ev-er reigns, And scat-ters night a-way.
When shall I see my Father's face, And in his bo-som rest?
Tho' Jordan's waves a-round me roll, Fear-less I'd launch a-way.

CHORUS.

We will rest in the fair and happy land, Just across on the evergreen shore, . .
by and by,   evergreen shore.

Sing the song of Moses and the Lamb, by and by, And dwell with Jesus evermore.

Bringing in the Sheaves.

Words from "Songs of Glory."

Geo. A. Minor.

1. Sowing in the morning, sowing seeds of kindness, Sowing in the noon-tide,
2. Sowing in the sunshine, sowing in the shadows, Fearing neither clouds nor
3. Go, then, ev-er weeping, sowing for the Master, Tho' the loss sustained our

and the dew-y eves; Waiting for the har-vest, and the time of reap-ing,
winter's chilling breeze; By and by the har-vest, and the la-bor end-ed,
spir-it oft-en grieves; When our weeping's over, he will bid us welcome,

CHORUS.

We shall come re-joic-ing, bringing in the sheaves. Bringing in the sheaves,

bringing in the sheaves,   bringing in the sheaves,
We shall come rejoicing,   Bringing in the sheaves,

bringing in the sheaves, We shall come rejoic-ing, bringing in the sheaves,

DO RE MI FA SO LA SI

Saviour, Blessed Saviour.

GODFREY THWING.   HAYDN.

1. Saviour, blessed Sav - iour, List- en whilst we sing, Hearts and voices
2. Near-er, ev - er near - er, Christ, we draw to thee, Deep in ad - o -
3. Great and ev-er great - er Are thy mercies here; True and ev-er-

rais - ing Prais- es 'to our King, All we have we of - fer:
ra - tion Bending low the knee: Thou for our re - demp - tion
last - ing Are thy glo - ries there, Where no pain, or sor - row,

All we hope to be, Bod - y, soul, and spir - it,
Cam'st on earth to die; Thou, that we might fol - low,
Toil, or care is known, Where the an - gel - le - gions

CHORUS.

All we yield to thee. Saviour, bless - ed Sav - iour,
Hast gone up on high.
Cir - cle round thy throne.

Listen whilst we sing, Hearts and voices rais- ing Praises to our King.

Clinging to the Cross.

FRANK GOULD.   JNO. R. SWENEY.

1. O, my heart is full of joy, for my sins are wash'd away, Clinging to the
2. I have laid my burden down, I have cast it on the Lord, Clinging to the
3. I have found the hallow'd peace which the world can never give, Clinging to the
4. I am happy in his love, I am safe beneath his care, Clinging to the

cross of Je - sus; I am trusting more and more in his mercy ev'ry day,
cross of Je - sus; I can now believe and claim ev'ry promise in his word,
cross of Jesus; I have promised by his grace while he spares me I will live
cross of Jesus; Tho' temptations I shall meet they shall never harm me there,

CHORUS.

Clinging to the cross of Je - sus. Cling-ing to the cross, where his

blood was shed for me, Clinging to the cross, where the flowing stream I see,

Clinging to the cross, where I come on bended knee; Blessed, blessed cross of Jesus!

DO RE MI FA SO LA SI

Tell Me the Story of Jesus.

Fanny J. Crosby.   Jno. R. Sweney.

1. Tell me the sto - ry of Je - sus, Write on my heart ev-'ry word,
2. Fast-ing, a - lone in the des - ert, Tell of the days that he passed,
3. Tell of the cross where they nailed him, Writhing in anguish and pain,

Chorus.—Tell me the sto - ry of Je - sus, Write on my heart ev-'ry word,

Fine.

Tell me the sto - ry most pre - cious, Sweetest that ev - er was heard;
How for our sins he was tempt - ed, Yet was triumphant at last;
Tell of the grave where they laid him, Tell how he liv - eth a - gain;

Tell me the sto - ry most pre - cious, Sweetest that ev - er was heard.

Tell how the an- gels, in cho - rus, Sang as they welcomed his birth,—
Tell of the years of his la - bor, Tell of the sorrows he bore,
Love in that sto - ry, so ten - der, Clear-er than ev - er I see;

D.C.

Glo - ry to God in the high - est! Peace and good tidings to earth.
He was despised and af- flict - ed, Homeless, re- ject- ed and poor.
Stay, let me weep while you whisper, Love paid the ransom for me.

Copyright, 1880, by John J. Hood.

DO RE MI FA SO LA SI

108   Rise, and Let Me In.

W. A. O.
Andante.   "Behold, I stand at the door and knock."—Rev. iii: 20.   N E. Townsend.

pp   *cres.*

1. Lo! a stranger standing there, Knocking, knocking at the door,
2. 'Tis thy Sav-iour wait-ing there, Knocking, knocking at the door,
3. Hear the Sav-iour call to - day, Knocking, knocking at the door,
4. Shall thy Saviour plead in vain, Knocking, knocking at the door?

pp   *cres.*

Love - ly stranger! wond'rous fair! Knocking, knocking at the door;
Call - ing thee, O wan - der - er, Knocking, knocking at the door;
Do not grieve thy Lord a - way, Knocking, knocking at the door.
Will you slight his call a - gain, Knocking, knocking at the door?

cres.   *cres.*

Wait-ing, oh, so pa - tient-ly! Call - ing, oh, so ten - der - ly!
Pleading, oh, so earn - est - ly! Striv-ing, oh, so faith - ful - ly!
Wea -ry, worn, and troub-led breast, Tempt-ed one, with care op - prest,
Will you heed his earn - est plea? "Heav - y la - den, come to me."

Op - en now thy heart to me; Oh, rise, and let me in.
'Tis thy Sav-iour calls to thee; Oh, rise, and let me in.
I will give thy spir - it rest; Oh, rise, and let me in.
Rest and peace I give to thee; Oh, rise, and let me in.

Entire Consecration.

FRANCES RIDLEY HAVERGAL. Chorus by W. J. K. WM. J. KIRKPATRICK.

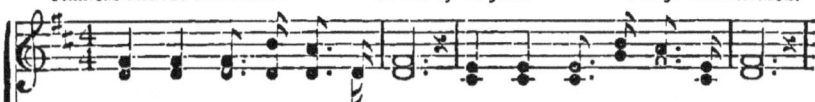

1. Take my life, and let it be Con - se - crat - ed, Lord, to thee;
2. Take my feet, and let them be Swift and beau - ti - ful for thee;
3. Take my lips, and let them be Filled with mes - sag - es for thee;
4. Take my moments and my days, Let them flow in endless praise;

Take my hands and let them move At the impulse of thy love.
Take my voice and let me sing Al - ways, on - ly, for my King.
Take my sil - ver and my gold,— Not a mite would I withhold.
Take my in - tel - lect, and use Ev - 'ry power as thou shalt choose.

CHORUS.

{ Wash me in the Saviour's precious blood, the precious blood,
{ Cleanse me in its pu - ri - fy - ing flood, the healing flood, } Lord, I give to

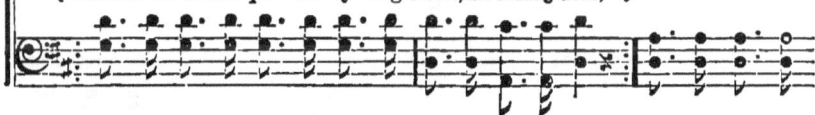

thee, my life and all, to be, Thine, henceforth, e - ter - nal - ly.

5 Take my will, and make it thine;
It shall be no longer mine;
Take my heart.—it is thine own,—
It shall be thy royal throne.

6 Take my love,—my Lord, I pour
At thy feet its treasure-store!
Take myself, and I will be
Ever, only, all for thee!

When the King comes in.

J. E. Landor.   Rev. E. S. Lorenz.

1. Call'd to the feast by the King are we, Sit-ting, perhaps, where his
2. Crowns on the head where the thorns have been, Glo-ri-fied he who once
3. Like lightning's flash will that instant show Things hidden long from both
4. Joy-ful his eye shall on each one rest Who is in white wedding

peo-ple be: How will it fare, then, with thee and me,
died for men; Splendid the vis-ion be-fore us then,
friend and foe, Just what we are ev-'ry one will know,
gar-ments dressed—Ah! well for us if we stand the test,

REFRAIN.

When the King comes in? When the King comes in, brother, When the King comes

in! . How will it fare with thee and me When the King comes in?

From "Songs of Grace," by per.

DO RE MI FA SO LA SI

Redeemed.

Fanny J. Crosby.   Wm. J. Kirkpatrick.

1. Redeemed, how I love to proclaim it, Redeemed by the blood of the Lamb;
2. Redeemed, and so happy in Je - sus, No language my rapture can tell,
3. I think of my blessed Redeemer, I think of him all the day long,
4. I know I shall see in his beauty The King in whose law I de - light,
5. I know there's a crown that is waiting In yonder bright mansion for me,

Redeemed thro' his infi - nite mer - cy, His child and forev - er I am.
I know that the light of his presence With me doth continual - ly dwell.
I sing, for I cannot be si - lent, His love is the theme of my song.
Who loving - ly guardeth my footsteps, And giveth me songs in the night,
And soon, with the spirits made perfect, At home with the Lord I shall be.

REFRAIN.

Re - deemed,   re - deemed,   redeemed by the blood of the Lamb,
redeemed,   redeemed,

Re - deemed,   re - deemed,   His child and forev - er I am.
redeemed,   redeemed,

DO RE MI FA SO LA SI

112 **He Came to Save Me.**

HENRIETTA E. BLAIR.   WM. J. KIRKPATRICK.

1. When Je - sus laid his crown a - side, He came to save me;
2. In my poor heart he deigns to dwell, He came to save me;
3. With gen - tle hand he leads me still, He came to save me;
4. To him my faith with rap- ture clings, He came to save me;

When on the cross he bled and died, He came to save me.
O, praise his name, I know it well, He came to save me.
And trust-ing him I fear no ill, He came to save me.
To him my heart looks up and sings, He came to save me.

CHORUS.

I'm so glad, I'm so glad, I'm so glad that Jesus came, And grace is free,

I'm so glad, I'm so glad, I'm so glad that Jesus came, He came to save me.

Copyright, 1896, by Wm. J. Kirkpatrick.

Hark, Hark, My Soul.

Rev. F. W. Faber.

Arr. from C. C. Converse by Ira D. Sankey.

113

Moderato.

1. Hark, hark, my soul, angelic songs are swelling O'er earth's green fields and
2. Far, far away, like bells at evening pealing, The voice of Je - sus
3. Onward we go, for still we hear them singing, "Come, weary souls, for

ocean's wave-beat shore; How sweet the truth those blessed strains are telling
sounds o'er land and sea, And la - den souls by thousands meekly stealing,
Jesus bids you come;" And thro' the dark, its echoes sweetly ring-ing,

CHORUS.

Of that new life when sin shall be no more. Angels, sing on! your faithful watches
Kind Shepherd, turn their weary steps to thee.
The music of the Gospel leads us home.

keep-ing; Sing us sweet fragments of the songs above, Till morning's joy shall

end the night of weeping, And life's long shadows break in cloudless love.

Temple Songs-H

Behold, the Fields are White.

Rev. M. Lowrie Hofford.

Jno. R. Sweney.

1. Look up! behold, the fields are white, The harvest time is near; The summons of the
2. Look up! behold, the fields are white, The laborers are few, The gath'ring of the
3. Look up! behold, the fields are white, The Master soon will come, And carry with re-

Mas-ter falls Up-on the reaper's ear: Go forth in-to the gold-en grain And
har-vest must By grace depend on you · Go forth throughout the busy world, The
joicing heart His gathered trophies home; And can you stand with empty arms, While

bind the precious sheaves, And garner for the Lord of Hosts The harvest which he gives.
world of want and sin, And gather for the Lord of Hosts Its dying millions in.
glad-ly he receives From others in the harvest field A load of precious sheaves.

CHORUS.

Look up!   look up!   behold, the fields are white,   The harvest time is
Look up!   look up!   be-hold! be-hold! the fields are white, The har-vest

near,   The har-vest time is   near: Look up!   look up!   be-
time is near,   the har---vest   time is near: Look up!   look up!

From "Our Sabbath Home," by per.

Behold, the Fields are White.—CONCLUDED. 115

hold, the fields are white, Look up! behold, the fields are white, The harvest time is near.

I will Trust in Thee.

In answer to question of leader at Ocean Grove "Who will trust?"
many rose, saying, "I will."

W. H. G.   W. H. GEISTWEIT.

1. Blessed Saviour, my sal - vation, I will trust in thee;   I am saved from
2. Sanctify and cleanse me, Saviour, I will trust in thee;   Let me know thy
3. Here I stand and thee confessing, I will trust in thee;   Pour up-on my

CHORUS.

condemn - a -tion, I will trust in thee.   Yes, I will, yes, I will,
lov - ing fa - vor, I will trust in thee.
heart thy blessing, I will trust in thee.

I will trust in thee; Thou, my Strength and Song forever, I will trust in thee.

DO RE MI FA SO LA SI

Meet in the Morning.

H. E. BLAIR.   WM. J. KIRKPATRICK.

1. We are marching onward to the heavenly land, To meet each other in the morning;
2. We are trav'ling onward from a world of care, To meet each other in the morning;
3. We are trav'ling onward, and the way grows bright, We'll meet each other in, etc.,

We are pressing forward to the golden strand, Where joy will crown us in the morning.
Oh, the time is coming, we shall soon be there, And joy will crown us in the morning.
Where our friends are waiting, at the gate of life, And joy will crown us in the, etc.,

CHORUS.

In the morning, in the morning, We will gather with the faithful in the morning;

Where the night of sorrow shall be rolled away, And joy will crown us in the morning.

4 Where the hills are blooming on the
  other shore,
We'll meet each other in the morning!
Where the heart's deep longing will be
  felt no more,
And joy will crown us in the morning.

5 In the boundless rapture of a Saviours'
  love
We'll meet each other in the morning;
Then we'll sing his glory in the realms
  above,
And joy will crown us in the morning.

Mrs. C. N. Pickop.   Wm. J. Kirkpatrick.

1. Jesus, the rock on which my feet May safely and securely stand,
2. Jesus, the rock on which I build, The sure foundation, true and tried;
3. Jesus the rock stands firm, secure, Unyielding, tho' the storms may beat;
4. Jesus the rock, blest Saviour, thou Art all I want, and all I crave;

While all around me sinks and falls, And scatters like the crumbling sand.
Bright star of hope for   ruined man, Is Jesus Christ, the cruci - fied!
In this sure trust I   anchor fast, And find a blessed safe re - treat.
I trust in thee, for   well I know Thy mighty power alone can save.

CHORUS.

Jesus the rock, I cling to thee, Tho' waves and billows 'round me roll;

Jesus my hope, my on - ly plea, The stay and comfort of my soul.

118

He Comes.

FANNY J. CROSBY.

JNO. R. SWENEY.

1. Awake! awake! O Zion, lift thy voice! In the Lord thy God forevermore re-
2. He comes! he comes! the faithful watchmen cry; To the hills look up and wave the [banner

Fine.

joice; A-rise! arise! behold, the night is past, And the day has come at last;
high! He comes! he comes! with trumpet tongue proclaim Our redemption thro' his [name.

Let thy harp resound as once it rang In the grand old time of thy strength and prime,
Oh, the songs, glad songs that now we raise In the dear retreat where we love to meet,

When thy soul within thee sweetly sang, Trusting in the promise of the Lord.
In the house of prayer and joyous praise, Singing with the happy ones above.

Hark! O Zi-on, hear the joy-bells ring! Lo, he cometh, thy Redeemer-King!
Crown, oh, crown him, our Deliv'rer-King! Hail, oh, hail him, while our gifts we bring!

ril. *Use first four lines as Cho.*

D.C.

He shall reign all glorious, He shall reign victorious O'er the world from shore to shore.
All shall hear his story, All shall see his glory; He shall reign from shore to shore.

We Know Not Why.

SALLIE MARTIN.   JNO. R. SWENEY.

1. We know not why our path at times Is one of thorns and sad-ness,
2. We know not why our warning words Seem lost or dis-re-gard-ed,
3. We know not why our brightest hopes Like autumn leaves must perish,

Fine.

While oth-ers walk a-mid the smile Of con-stant joy and gladness.
While oth-ers reap, from day to day, The fruit of toil reward-ed.
Or why the hand of death removes The friends that most we cherish.

D.S.—Though heaven and earth should pass away, His truth shall stand forever!

CHORUS.   D.S.

But this we know, the Lord is just, His promise fail-eth nev-er;

4 We know not what our joy will be
   When, in the realms of glory,
   We at the Saviour's feet shall tell
   Redemption's wondrous story.

5 O then, content, we'll walk by faith,
   Our hearts his love possessing;
   We'll praise him for his mercies past,
   And trust for every blessing.

Do Something To-Day.

LANTA WILSON SMITH.   WM. J. KIRKPATRICK.

1. You're longing to work for the Master, Yet waiting for something to do;
2. Go rescue that wandering brother Who sinks 'neath his burden of woe,
3. Go sing happy songs of rejoicing With those who no sorrows have known;
4. O never, my brother, stand waiting, Be willing to do what you can;

You fancy the future is holding Some wonderful mission for you;
A single kind action may save him, If love and compassion you show;
Go weep with the heart-broken mourner, Go comfort the sad and the lone;
The humblest service is need -ed, To fill out the Father's great plan;

But while you are waiting the moments Are rapid-ly passing a - way;
Don't shrink from the vilest about you, If you can but lead them from sin;
From pitfalls and snares of the tempter Go rescue the thoughtless and wild:
Be earning your stars of rejoic - ing While earth-life is passing a - way;

O brother, awake from your dreaming, Do something for Jesus to - day.
For this is the grandest of missions,— Lost souls for the Master to win.
Go win from pale lips a 'God bless you,' Go brighten the life of a child.
Win some one to meet you in glo - ry,— Do something for Jesus to - day.

CHORUS.

Do something, do something, Do something for Jesus to - day ;
Do something, do something,

O brother, the moments are passing, Do something for Jesus to - day.

Jesus will Meet You There.

W. L. K.   W. Lewis Kane.

1. Come to Calv'ry's mount to - day, Je - sus will meet you there ;
Look and live without de - lay, Je - sus will meet you there.

CHORUS.

Come to Jesus, Don't stay away, my friend ; Come to Jesus, He calls to-day.

2 Rest beneath the hallowed cross,
Jesus will meet you there ;
Saving mercy gained for loss,
Jesus will meet you there.

3 Come and join his faithful band,
Jesus will meet you there ;
Take his mighty, helping hand,
Jesus will meet you there.

4 At the blessed mercy seat,
Jesus will meet you there ;
Come with this assurance sweet,
Jesus will meet you there.

5 You'll find rest in heaven at last,
Jesus will meet you there ;
And be happy with the blest,
Jesus will meet you there.

On the Road, Going Home.

P. J. OWENS.   WM. J. KIRKPATRICK.

1. We are go - ing home to glo - ry, Bright a - bode, bright a - bode!
2. We will call to those faint hearted, "Be of cheer, be of cheer;"
3. We will call to souls in blindness, "Come this way, come this way;"

And will gladly work for Je - sus, On the road, on the road.
And to pilgrims who have started, "Never fear, nev - er fear."
We will tell Christ's loving kindness, Ev - 'ry day, ev - 'ry day.

CHORUS.

For his mercy sought and found us, And his blood to service bound us;

So we'll work for all around us, On the road, go - ing home.

4 May our souls with love be yearning
  As we sing, as we sing;
  May our lamps be brightly burning,
  For the King, for the King.

5 We are waiting till his message
  Bids us come, bids us come;
  But we'll live and work for Jesus,
  Going home, going home.

Showers of Blessing.

"And I will cause the shower to come down in his season."
Ezekiel xxxiv. 26.

JENNIE GARNETT.   JNO. R. SWENEY.

1. Here in thy name we are gathered, Come and revive us, O Lord;
2. O that the showers of bless-ing Now on our souls may descend,
3. There shall be showers of blessing.—Promise that never can fail;
4. Showers of blessing,—we need them, Showers of blessing from thee;

"There shall be showers of bless-ing" Thou hast declared in thy word.
While at the footstool of mer - cy Pleading thy promise we bend!
Thou wilt regard our pe - ti - tion; Sure - ly our faith will pre - vail.
Showers of blessing,—oh, grant them; Thine all the glory shall be.

CHORUS.

Oh, gracious-ly hear us, Gracious-ly hear us, we pray:
gracious - ly hear us,

Pour from thy windows upon us Showers of blessing to - day.
Lord, pour up - on us

Triumph By and By.

Dr. C. R. BLACKALL.   H. R. PALMER. By per.

1. The prize is set before   us, To win his words implore us, The
2. We'll follow where he leadeth, We'll pasture where he feedeth, We'll
3. Our home is bright above   us, No tri - als dark to move us, But

eye of God is o'er us, From on high, from on high; His loving tones are calling,
yield to him who pleadeth From on high,   Then naught from him shall sever,
Jesus, dear, to love us, There on high, there on high; We'll give him best endeavor,

While sin is dark, appalling; 'Tis Jesus gently calling, He is nigh, he is nigh.
Our hope shall brighten ever, And faith shall fail us never, He is nigh, he is nigh.
And praise his name forever; His precious ones can never, Never die, never die.

CHORUS.

By and by   we shall meet him, By and by we shall greet him, And with

1st.
Jesus reign in glory, By and by, by and by;

2d.
Jesus reign in glory, By and by.

Are You Washed in the Blood?

E. A. H.   Rev. E. A. Hoffman. By per.

1. Have you been to Jesus for the cleansing power? Are you washed in the
2. Are you walking dai - ly by the Saviour's side? Are you washed in the
3. When the Bridegroom cometh will your robes be white, Pure and white in the
4. Lay a- side the garments that are stained with sin, And be washed in the

blood of the Lamb? Are you ful- ly trusting in his grace this hour? Are you
blood of the Lamb? Do you rest each moment in the Cru - ci- fied? Are you
blood of the Lamb? Will your soul be ready for the mansions bright, And be
blood of the Lamb? There's a fountain flowing for the soul unclean, O be

CHORUS.

washed in the blood of the Lamb? Are you washed in the
Are you washed

blood, In the soul-cleansing blood of the Lamb? Are your
in the blood, of the Lamb?

garments spotless? are they white as snow? Are you washed in the blood of the Lamb?

Waiting at the Pool.

Rev. A. J. Hough.　　　　　　　　　　　　Wm. G. Fischer　By per.

1. Thousands stand to-day in sorrow, Waiting at the pool; Saying they will
2. Souls your filthy garments wearing, Waiting at the pool; Hearts your heavy
3. Thousands once were standing near you, Waiting at the pool; Come their voices
4. Mother leaves the son, the daughter, Waiting at the pool; Calls to them a-
5. Step in boldly—death may smite you, Waiting at the pool: Jesus may no

wash to-morrow, Waiting at the pool; Oth- ers step in left and right,
bur- den bearing, Waiting at the pool; Can it be you nev- er heard,
back to cheer you, Waiting at the pool; Back from Canaan's happy shore,
cross the water, Waiting at the pool; You can nev - er more embrace
more invite you, Waiting at the pool; Faith is near you, take her hand,

Wash their stained garments white, Leav- ing you　in sorrow's night,
Jesus long a - go hath stirred-The wa - ters with his might- y word,
Sor - rows past and la - bor o'er, Where they stand in tears no more,
Moth - er or be - hold her face, If　you keep the lep - er's place.
Seek with her the bet - ter land, And　no long - er doubting stand

Waiting at the pool, Waiting, wait- ing, waiting at the pool.

FRANK GOULD. JNO R. SWENEY.

1. At the cross I found my Saviour, And my boasting there shall be,
2. At the cross I cried for mer - cy, Jesus heard my humble prayer;
3. At the cross he gave me com- fort, In my darkest hour he came,
4. When among the just made perfect My Redeem- er I shall see,

For my man - y sins are pardoned Through the blood he shed for me.
I was wretched, weak, and helpless, Till on him I cast my care.
And my faith looked up and saw him, Hal- le - lu - jah to his name!
I will tell, through endless a- ges, What his love has done for me!

CHORUS.

O my soul in him rejoic - es, And the world I count but dross,—

I am walk-ing, dai- ly walking In the shadow of the cross.

Glory to God, Hallelujah!

FANNY J. CROSBY.   WM. J. KIRKPATRICK.

1. We are nev-er, nev-er wea-ry of the grand old song; Glo-ry to
2. We are lost a-mid the rapture of redeem-ing love; Glo-ry to
3. We are go-ing to a palace that is built of gold; Glo-ry to
4. There we'll shout redeeming mercy in a glad, new song; Glo-ry to

God, hal-le-lu-jah! We can sing it loud as ever, with our faith more strong:
God, hal-le-lu-jah! We are rising on its pinions to the hills a-bove:
God, hal-le-lujah! Where the King in all his splendor we shall soon behold:
God, hallelujah! There we'll sing the praise of Jesus with the blood-wash'd throng:

Fine. CHORUS.

Glo-ry to God, hal-le-lu-jah! O, the children of the Lord have a

right to shout and sing, For the way is grow-ing bright, and our

D.S.

souls are on the wing; We are going by and by to the palace of a King!

Make Room for Jesus.

"There was no room for them at the inn."
Luke ii. 7.

Rev. ALEX. CLARK, D D

WM. G FISCHER.

1. Make room for Je - sus! room! sad heart, Beguiled and sick of sin;
2. Make room for Je - sus! room! make room! His hand is at the door;
3. Make room for Je - sus! soul of mine, He waits re-sponse to-day;
4. Make room for Je - sus! by and by, 'Midst saint and ser - a - phim,

Bid ev - 'ry a - lien guest de-part, And rise and let him in.
He comes to ban - ish guilt and gloom, And bless thee more and more.
His smile is peace, his grace, di-vine, Oh, turn him not a - way.
He'll welcome to his throne on high The soul that welcomed him.

CHORUS.

Make room, sad heart, make room, make room! Bid a-lien guests de - part,

Oh, let the Mas - ter in, sad heart; A-rise, make room, make room!

By permission.

Temple Songs-I

130   Meet me There.

HENRIETTA E. BLAIR.   WM. J. KIRKPATRICK.

1. On the happy, golden shore, Where the faithful part no more, When the
2. Here our fondest hopes are vain, Dearest links are rent in twain; But in
3. Where the harps of angels ring, And the blest for-ev-er sing, In the

storms of life are o'er, Meet me there; Where the night dissolves away Into
heav'n no throb of pain, Meet me there; By the river sparkling bright, In the
palace of the King, Meet me there; Where in sweet communion blend Heart with

Fine.

pure and perfect day, I am going home to stay, Meet me there.
ci - ty of delight, Where our faith is lost in sight, Meet me there.
heart, and friend with friend, In a world that ne'er shall end, Meet me there.

D.S.—happy golden shore, Where the faithful part no more, Meet me there.

CHORUS.

Meet me there,   Meet me there,   Where the tree of life is

D.S.

blooming, Meet me there;   When the storms of life are o'er, On the

Meet me there;

A little Talk with Jesus.

WM. G. FISCHER.

1. A lit-tle talk with Je-sus, How it smooths the rugged road!
2. Ah, this is what I'm wanting, His love-ly face to see;
3. I can-not live without him, Nor would I if I could;
4. So I'll wait a lit-tle long-er, Till his appoint-ed time,

How it seems to help me on-ward, When I faint beneath my load;
And I'm not a-fraid to say it, I know he's wanting me.
He is my dai-ly por-tion, My med-i-cine and food.
And a-long the upward path-way My pil-grim feet shall climb.

When my heart is crushed with sorrow, And my eyes with tears are dim,
He gave his life a ran-som, To make me all his own,
He is al-to-geth-er love-ly; None can with him com-pare;
There, in my Father's dwell-ing, Where man-y mansions be,

There is naught can yield me comfort Like a lit-tle talk with him.
And he'll ne'er forget his prom-ise To me, his purchased one.
Chief-est among ten thousand, And fair-est of the fair.
I shall sweetly talk with Je-sus, And he will talk with me.

By permission.

On let us go.

FANNY J. CROSBY. WM. J. KIRKPATRICK.

1. On let us go where the val-ley of Ed - en fair Blooms on the
2. On let us go where the beauti- ful realms above Ring with the
3. On let us go where the weary and toil-oppressed Soon shall for-
4. On let us go where the loving and loved shall meet, Meet on the

bank of the riv - er; On where the fields, in the beautiful robe they wear,
time-honored sto - ry: Saved thro' the might of a blessed Redeemer's love,
get ev -'ry sor - row; On where the soul to a happy and golden rest
bank of the riv - er; There shall they sing at the blessed Redeemer's feet

CHORUS.

Wave in the sunlight for - ev - er. On let us go,
His be the praise and the glo - ry.
Wakes in e - ter - ni- ty's mor- row. On, march on, to the beauti - ful land we go,
Songs that shall echo for - ev - er.

On let us go, On let us
On, march on, to the beau - ti - ful land we go, On, march on, where the

go, On where the hap - py ones are call - ing.
riv - ers of pleasure flow,

A Shelter in the Time of Storm. 133

Words arranged.   "My God is the Rock of my refuge."—Ps. xciv : 22.   Ira D. Sankey.

1. The Lord's our Rock, in him we hide, A shelter in the time of storm;
2. A shade by day defence by night, A shelter in the time of storm;
3. The raging storms may round us beat, A shelter in the time of storm;
4. O Rock divine, O Refuge dear, A shelter in the time of storm;

Secure whatev - er ill be - tide, A shelter in the time of storm.
No fears alarm, no foes af-fright, A shelter in the time of storm.
We'll nev - er leave our safe retreat, A shelter in the time of storm.
Be thou our helper ev - er near, A shelter in the time of storm.

CHORUS.

Oh, Jesus is a Rock in a weary land, A weary land, a weary land; Oh,

Jesus is a Rock in a weary land, A shelter in the time of storm.

134 Only a Beam of Sunshine.

FANNY J. CROSBY.   JNO. R. SWENEY.

1. On-ly a beam of sun-shine, But oh, it was warm and bright; The
2. On-ly a beam of sun-shine That in-to a dwell-ing crept, Where,
3. On-ly a word for Je-sus! Oh, speak it in his dear name; To

heart of a wea-ry trav-'ler Was cheered by its wel-come sight.
o-ver a fad-ing rose-bud, A moth-er her vig-il kept.
per-ish-ing souls a-round you The message of love pro-claim.

On-ly a beam of sun-shine That fell from the arch a-bove, And
On-ly a beam of sun-shine That smiled thro' her falling tears, And
Go, like the faith-ful sun-beam, Your mission of joy ful-fil; Re-

ten-der-ly, soft-ly whispered A mes-sage of peace and love.
showed her the bow of prom-ise, For-got-ten perhaps for years.
member the Saviour's prom-ise, That he will be with you still.

CHORUS.

On-ly a word for Je-sus, On-ly a whispered prayer

DO RE MI FA SO LA SI

O - ver some grief-worn spir - it May rest like a sun-beam fair.

The New Name.

J. E. H.

J. E. HALL.

1. We shall have a new name in that land, In that land, that sunny, sunny land,
2. We'll receive it in a pure white stone, And no one will know the name therein;
3. Don't you wonder what that name will be, Sweeter far than aught on earth can be,

Cho.—We shall have a new name in that land, In that land, that sunny, sunny land,

Fine.

When we meet the bright angelic band, In that sunny land. A new name, a
Only unto him who hath 'tis known, When we're free from sin. A white stone, a
We will be quite satisfied when we Shall that new name know. I won- der, I

When we meet the bright angelic band, In that sunny land.

D. C.

new name We'll receive up there; A new name, a new name, All who enter there.
white stone We'll receive up there; A white stone, a white stone, All who enter there.
won- der What that name will be, I wonder, I wonder, What he'll give to me.

My Shepherd.

Rev. Joseph H. Martin.   Ps. xxiii.   Wm. J. Kirkpatrick.

1. The Lord . . . is my shep - - - herd, my keep - - er and
2. Whenev - - - er I wan - - - der, and leave . . the true

1. The Lord is my shepherd, my keeper and guide, The Lord is my shepherd, my
2. Whenev - er I wan - der, and leave the true way, When-ev - er I wan - der, and

guide, . . . My wants . . . he'll sup- ply, . . . and for
way, ... And like . . . a lost sheep . . . from the

keep- er and guide, My wants he'll supply, and for me he'll provide, My
leave the true way, And like a lost sheep from the flock go a - stray, And

me . . . . he'll pro- vide; . . . In midst . . of green
flock . . . go a - stray; . . My soul . . . he re-

wants he'll sup- ply, and for me he'll provide; In midst of green pastures he
like a lost sheep from the flock go a - stray; My soul he restores to the

pas - - - - tures he makes - - me to lie, . . . Be-
stores . . . to the path . . . that is right, . . . He

makes me to lie, In midst of green pastures he makes me to lie, Be-
path that is right, My soul he restores to the path that is right, He

DO RE MI FA SO LA SI

My Shepherd.—CONCLUDED.

side . . the still wa - - ters that gen - - tly pass by. . .
leads . . me in safe - - ty, I walk - - in his light. .

side the still waters that gently pass by, That gently, that gently pass by.
leads me in safe- ty, I walk in his light, In safety I walk in his light.

CHORUS.

My Shepherd will provide, what - ev - er may be-tide; I am se-

cure, For his promise is sure, The Lord will pro - vide.

3 When called to surrender my faltering breath,
And pass through the vale of the shadow of death,
The presence of Jesus will brighten the tomb,
With hope and with gladness dispelling its gloom.
    With gladness dispelling its gloom.

4 For me his free bounty a table has spread;
And blessings unmeasured he pours on my head;
My cup with abundance and joy overflows;
He dries all my tears, and he heals all my woes.
    He heals all my woes, all my woes.

5 His goodness and mercy shall crown all my days,
My mouth shall be filled with thanksgiving and praise;
I'll dwell in his temple of glory above,
And sing evermore of his grace and his love.
    And sing of his grace and his love.

137

137 Little Ones Like Me.

1. Je- sus, when he left the sky, And for sinners came to die, In his
2. Mothers then the Saviour sought In the places where he taught, And to
3. Did the Saviour say them nay? No, he kindly bade them stay, Suffered
4. 'Twas for them his life he gave, To redeem them from the grave, Jesus

CHORUS.

mer-cy passed not by Little ones like me. Little ones, little ones,
him the children brought, Little ones like me.
none to turn a - way Little ones like me.
now will gladly save Little ones like me.

"Suffer them to come," said he; Jesus loves the little ones, Little ones like me.

Copyright, 1880, by John J. Hood.

138 Touch and Cleanse Me.

MARY F. MARSH.   Matt. viii. 3.   WARREN W. BENTLEY.

1. Touch and cleanse me, blessed Sav- iour, I am wea - ry of my sin;
2. Touch and cleanse me, blessed Sav- iour, Humbly now my guilt I own;
3. Touch and cleanse me, blessed Sav- iour, I am poor, and weak, and blind;
4. Thou dost cleanse me blessed Sav- iour, Light is streaming from a- bove;

By permission of E. T. Gordon & Son.

138

Touch and Cleanse Me.—CONCLUDED.

Fine.

I am long-ing for thy fa - vor, Longing to be pure within.
Oh, be-stow thy pard'ning fa - vor! Thou canst save me, thou alone.
Grant me now thy lov-ing fa - vor, Let me now sal - vation find.
Now I feel thy pard'ning fa - vor, Oh, my soul is full of love.

D.S.—Touch and cleanse me, touch and cleanse me, Jesus, save me or I die.
D.S.—Thou dost cleanse me, thou dost cleanse me, Glory be to God on high.

REFRAIN.

D.S.

Touch and cleanse me, touch and cleanse me, Listen to my fee-ble cry,
4th v. Thou dost cleanse me, thou dost cleanse me, Thou hast heard my feeble cry,

139   The Morning Light.

SAMUEL F. SMITH.

Tune, WEBB. 7, 6.
Fine.

D.S.

1 The morning light is breaking;
The darkness disappears;
The sons of earth are waking
To penitential tears;
Each breeze that sweeps the ocean
Brings tidings from afar,
Of nations in commotion,
Prepared for Zion's war.

2 See heathen nations bending
Before the God we love,
And thousand hearts ascending
In gratitude above;
While sinners, now confessing,
The gospel call obey,
And seek the Saviour's blessing,
A nation in a day.

3 Blest river of salvation,
Pursue thine onward way;
Flow thou to every nation,
Nor in thy richness stay:
Stay not till all the lowly
Triumphant reach their home:
Stay not till all the holy
Proclaim, "The Lord is come!"

140 Leaning on Jesus.

Rev. W. F. Crafts.   Wm. J. Kirkpatrick.

1. Wea-ry with walking a - lone, Long heav-y - laden with sin;
2. Fearing to stand for my Lord, Trembling for weakness in prayer;

Toil-ing all night with-out Christ,—Rest for my soul shall I win,
Yet on the bo-som di - vine Los - ing each sor-row and fear,

CHORUS.

Lean - ing on Je - sus, I walk - at his side; . .
Leaning on Je-sus, in him I a - bide.   Leaning on Je - sus, I walk at his side;

Lean - - ing on Je - - sus, I trust him, my Shepherd and Guide.
Leaning on Je- sus, what-ev- er be - tide,

3 Anxious no longer for self,
   Shrinking no longer from pain;
Leaning on Jesus alone,
   He all my care will sustain.
     Leaning on Jesus, etc.

4 Leaning, I walk in " The Way,"
   Leaning, " The Truth " I shall know;
Leaning on heart-throbs of Christ,
   Safe into " Life " I may go.
     Leaning on Jesus, etc.

From " Leaflet Gems, No. 2," by per.

Come and See.

Charles H. Elliott. Jno. R. Sweney.

1. There is pardon sweet, at the Master's feet, Come and see, O come and see;
2. There's an easy yoke that you all may bear, Come and see, O come and see;
3. There's a healing balm for the weary breast, Come and see, O come and see;
4. There's a life beyond, 'tis a life di-vine, Come and see, O come and see;

CHORUS.

There's a song of peace that shall never cease, Come, O come and see.
There's a ho-ly joy that you all may share, Come, O come and see.
There's a tranquil peace and a sa-cred rest, Come, O come and see.
And the light of faith on your path will shine, Come, O come and see.

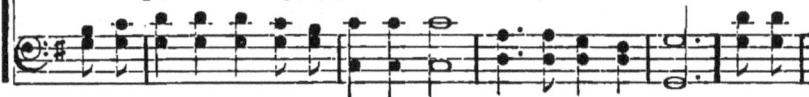

In the precious, precious blood of Je-sus Washed a-way your sins may be;

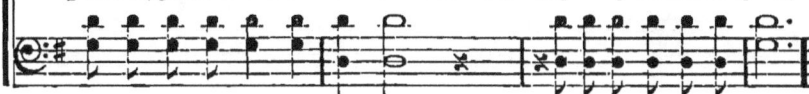

You may plunge just now in its cleansing flood,—Come, will you come and see.

Copyright, 1886, by John J. Hood.

DO RE MI FA SO LA SI.

142 Wont You Love My Jesus?

SALLIE SMITH.   JNO. R. SWENEY.

1. I have found a friend di - vine, Wont you love him too?
2. Oh, how dear his name to me, Wont you love him too?
3. Heav - y - lad - en, care - oppressed, Wont you love him too?
4. Cast your bur - den at his feet, Wont you love him too?

I am his and he is mine, Wont you love him too?
None can save your soul but he, Wont you love him too?
How he longs to give you rest, Wont you love him too?
There is par - don pure and sweet, Wont you love him too?

CHORUS.

Wont you love my Je - sus, My pre-cious, precious Je - sus?

Wont you love my Je - sus? He is waiting now for you.

DO RE MI FA SO LA SI

Holy, Holy, Holy!

"They rest not day and night, saying, Holy, holy, holy, Lord God Almighty."—Rev. iv. 8.

REGINALD HEBER.   JOHN B. DYKES.,

1. Ho - ly, ho - ly, ho - ly! Lord God Al - might - y!
2. Ho - ly, ho - ly, ho - ly! all the saints a - dore thee,
3. Ho - ly, ho - ly, ho - ly! though the darkness hide thee,
4. Ho - ly, ho - ly, ho - ly! Lord God Al - migh - ty!

Grate - ful - ly a - dor - ing our song shall rise to thee;
Cast - ing down their golden crowns a - round the glass - y sea;
Though the eyes of sin - ful man thy glo - ry may not see,
All thy works shall praise thy name in earth, and sky, and sea;

Ho - ly, ho - ly, ho - ly! mer - ci - ful and might - y!
Cher - u - bim and se - ra - phim fall - ing down be - fore thee,
On - ly thou art ho - ly, there is none be - side thee
Ho - ly, ho - ly, ho - ly! mer - ci - ful and might - y!

God in three per - sons, bless - ed Trin - i - ty!
Which wert and art and ev - er - more. shall be.
Per - fect in power, in love and pur - i - ty.
God in three per - sons, bless - ed Trin - i - ty!

The Firm Foundation.

GEORGE KEITH.

Tune, PORTUGUESE HYMN.

1. How firm a foundation, ye saints of the Lord, Is laid for your
2. "Fear not, I am with thee, O be not dismayed, For I am thy
3. "When thro' the deep waters I call thee to go, The riv - ers of
4. "When thro' fie - ry tri - als thy path - way shall lie, My grace all suf -

faith in his ex - cel - lent word ' What more can he say, than to
God, I will still give thee aid; I'll strengthen thee, help thee, and
sor - row shall not o - ver - flow; For I will be with thee thy
fi - cient, shall be thy sup - ply, The flame shall not hurt thee; I

you he hath said, To you, who for re - fuge to Je - sus have
cause thee to stand, Up - held by my gracious, om - ni - po - tent
tri - als to bless, And sanc - ti - fy to thee thy deepest dis -
on - ly de - sign Thy dross to consume, and thy gold to re -

fled? To you, who for re - fuge to Je - sus have fled?
hand, Up - held by my gracious, om - ni - po - tent hand.
tress, And sanc - ti - fy to thee thy deep - est dis - tress.
fine, Thy dross to consume, and thy gold to re - fine.

5 "E'en down to old age all my people shall prove
shall prove   [love;
My sovereign, eternal, unchangeable
And when hoary hairs shall their tem-
ples adorn,   [be borne.
Like lambs they shall still in my bosom

6 "The soul that on Jesus hath leaned
for repose,
I will not, I will not desert to his foes;
That soul, though all hell should en-
deavor to shake,
I'll never, no never, no never forsake!"

Redeemed, Praise the Lord.

145

ABBIE MILLS. WM. J. KIRKPATRICK.

1. O happy day! what a Sav-iour is mine! I am redeemed, praise the Lord!
2. O clap your hands, all ye people of God, I am redeemed, praise the Lord!
3. Thanks be to God for the great vict'ry given, I am redeemed, praise the Lord!
4. Glory to God, I would shout ev-ermore, I am redeemed, praise the Lord!

Fine.

All to his pleasure I glad-ly re-sign, I am redeemed, praise the Lord!
Let ev'ry tongue speak his mercy abroad, I am redeemed, praise the Lord!
Now I am free; ev'ry chain has been riven,—I am redeemed, praise the Lord!
O for a voice that could reach ev'ry shore, I am redeemed, praise the Lord!

Key C.

Jesus has taken my burden away; Jesus has turned all my night into day;
His loving-kindness is better than gold; He doth bestow more than my cup can hold;
Out of the pit, and the mire, and the clay, Jesus has borne me in triumph away;
Help me, ye ransom'd, awake, ev'ry string, Let earth rejoice and the whole heavens ring,

Use first four lines as Chorus. D. C.

Jesus has come to my heart,—come to stay,—I am redeemed, praise the Lord!
Wondrous Salvation, that ne'er can be told,—I am redeemed, praise the Lord!
Safe on the rock I am standing to-day,—I am redeemed, praise the Lord!
While we the chorus u-ni-ted-ly sing, I am redeemed, praise the Lord!

Copyright, 1886, by John J. Hood. *Temple Songs-K*

DO RE MI FA SO LA SI

Trusting in the Promise.

Rev. H. B. HARTZLER.   E. S. LORENZ.

1. { I have found repose for my weary soul
     And a harbor safe when the billows roll, } Trusting in the promise of the Saviour;

2. { I will sing my song as the days go by,
     And rejoice in hope, while I live or die, } Trusting in the promise of the Saviour;

3. { O the peace and joy of the life I live,
     O the strength and love only God can give, } Trusting in the promise of the Saviour;

{ I will fear no foe in the deadly strife,
  I will bear my lot in the toil of life, } Trusting in the promise of the Saviour;

{ I can smile at grief, and abide in pain,
  And the loss of all shall be highest gain, } Trusting in the promise of the Saviour;

{ Whosoever will may be saved to-day,
  And begin to walk in the holy way, } Trusting in the promise of the Saviour;

REFRAIN.

Resting on his mighty arm forev - er, Never from his loving heart to sever,

I will rest by grace in his strong embrace, Trusting in the promise of the Saviour;

From "Songs of Refreshing," by per.

Come to Jesus. 147

J. H. S.

Rev. J. H. STOCKTON.

1. Come, ev-'ry soul by sin oppressed, There's mercy with the Lord;
2. For Je-sus shed his pre-cious blood Rich blessings to be-stow;
3. Yes, Je-sus is the Truth, the Way, That leads you in-to rest;

:S:

Fine.

And he will sure-ly give you rest, By trusting in his word.
Plunge now in-to the crim-son flood That washes white as snow.
Be-lieve in him, with-out de-lay, And you are ful-ly blest.

D. S.—He will save you, he will save you, He will save you now.

CHORUS.

D. S.

Come to Je-sus, come to Je-sus, Come to Je-sus now!

Second Chorus.

On-ly trust him, on-ly trust him, On-ly trust him now;

4 O Jesus, blessed Jesus, dear,
I'm coming now to thee;
Since thou hast made the way so clear,
And full salvation free.

5 Come, then, and join this holy band,
And on to glory go;
To dwell in that celestial land
Where joys immortal flow.

Come, Humble Sinner.

Tune above.

1 COME, humble sinner, in whose breast
A thousand thoughts revolve,
Come, with your guilt and fear opprest,
And make this last resolve:—

2 I'll go to Jesus, though my sin
Like mountains round me close;
I know his courts, I'll enter in,
Whatever may oppose.

3 Prostrate I'll lie before his throne,
And there my guilt confess;

I'll tell him I'm a wretch undone,-
Without his sovereign grace.

4 Perhaps he will admit my plea,
Perhaps will hear my prayer;
But, if I perish, I will pray,
And perish only there.

5 I can but perish, if I go;
I am resolved to try:
For if I stay away I know
I must forever die. —EDMUND JONES.

Let Him In.

Rev. J. B. Atchinson.   E. O. Excell.

1. There's a stranger at the door,   Let   him in,
2. O-pen now to him your heart,   Let   him in,
3. Hear you now his lov-ing voice?   Let   him in,
4. Now admit the heavenly Guest,   Let   him in,

Let the Saviour in,   let the Saviour in,

He has been there oft be - fore,   Let   him in;
If you wait he will de - part,   Let   him in;
Now, oh, now make him your choice,   Let   him in,
He will make for you a   feast,   Let   him in,

Let the Saviour in,   let the Saviour in,

Let him in ere he is gone, Let him in the Ho - ly One.
Let him in, he is your Friend, He your soul will sure de - fend,
He is stand-ing at the door, Joy to you he will re - store,
He will speak your sins for-given, And when earth ties all are riven,

Je-sus Christ, the Father's Son,   Let   him in.
He will keep you to the end,   Let   him in.
And his name you will a - dore,   Let   him in.
He will take you home to heaven,   Let   him in.

Let the Saviour in.   let the Saviour in.

"Mine are thine and thine are mine."
John xvii. 10.

"London Hymn Book."   A. J. GORDON. By per.

1. My Je - sus, I love thee, I know thou art mine,
2. I love thee be - cause thou have first lov - ed me,
3. I will love thee in life, I'll love thee in death,
4. In man - sions of glo - ry and end - less delight,

For thee all the fol - lies of sin I re - sign;
And pur - chased my par - don on Cal - va - ry's tree;
And praise thee as long as thou lend - est me breath;
I'll ev - er a - dore thee in heav - en so bright;

My gra - cious Re - deem - er, my Sav - iour art thou,
I love thee for wear - ing the thorns on thy brow;
And say, when the death - dew lies cold on my brow,
I'll sing with the glit - ter - ing crown on my brow,

If ev - er I loved thee, my Je - sus, 'tis now.

150

Whiter than Snow.

"Wash me, and I shall be whiter than snow"
Psalm li. 7.

JAMES NICHOLSON.   WM. G. FISCHER. By per.

1. Lord Je-sus, I long to be per-fect-ly whole; I want thee for-
2. Lord Je-sus, look down from thy throne in the skies And help me to
3. Lord Je-sus, for this I most humbly en-treat; I wait, blessed
4. Lord Je-sus, thou se-est I pa-tient-ly wait; Come now, and with

ev - er, to live in my soul; Break down ev'ry i - dol, cast
make a com-plete sac - ri - fice; I give up my - self, and what-
Lord, at thy cru - ci - fied feet, By faith, for my cleansing, I
in me a new heart cre - ate; To those who have sought thee, thou

out ev'ry foe; Now wash me, and I shall be whit-er than snow.
ev - er I know—Now wash me, and I shall be whit-er than snow.
see thy blood flow—Now wash me, and I shall be whit-er than snow.
nev - er said'st No—Now wash me, and I shall be whit-er than snow.

CHORUS.

Whiter than snow, yes, whiter than snow;
Now wash me, and I shall be whiter than snow.

151 I am Coming to the Cross.

Rev. Wm. McDonald.   John vi. 37.   Wm. G. Fischer. By per.

1. I am com - ing to the cross; I · am poor, and weak, and blind;
2. Long my heart has sighed for thee, Long has e - vil reigned within:
3. Here I give my all to thee, Friends, and time, and earthly store;

CHO.— I am trust - ing, Lord, in thee, Blest Lamb of Cal - va - ry;

D. C.

I am count - ing all but dross, I shall full sal - va - tion find.
Je - sus sweet - ly speaks to me.— "I will cleanse you from all sin."
Soul and bo - dy thine to be,— Whol - ly thine for ev - er-more.

Humbly at thy cross I bow, Save me, Je - sus, save me now.

4 In thy promises I trust,
Now I feel the blood applied:
I am prostrate in the dust,
I with Christ am crucified.

5 Jesus comes! he fills my soul!
Perfected in him I am;
I am every whit made whole;
Glory, glory to the Lamb.

152 Rest for the Weary.   Rev. Wm. McDonald.

Rev. S. G. Harmer.

1. In the Christian's home in glo - ry There re-mains a land of rest;
2. Pain or sickness ne'er shall en - ter, Grief nor woe my lot shall share;
3. Death itself shall then be vanquished, And his sting shall be withdrawn:
4. Sing, oh, sing, ye heirs of glo - ry; Shout your triumph as you go;

There my Saviour's gone be - fore me, To ful - fil my soul's request.
But in that ce - les - tial cen - tre, I a crown of life shall wear.
Shout for gladness, O ye ransomed! Hail with joy the ris - ing morn.
Zi - on's gates will o - pen for you, You shall find an entrance through.

CHORUS.

There is rest for the wea - ry, There is rest for the
On the oth - er side of Jor - dan, In the sweet fields of

wea - ry, There is rest for the wea - ry, There is rest for you—
E - den, Where the tree of life is blooming, There is rest for you.

151

153. Come, Ye Disconsolate.

THOMAS MOORE, alt., and THOS. HASTINGS.   SAMUEL WEBBE.

1. Come, ye disconsolate, where'er ye languish; Come to the mercy-seat, fervently kneel;

Here bring your wounded hearts, here tell your anguish;
Earth has no sorrow that heaven cannot heal.

2 Joy of the desolate, light of the straying,
Hope of the penitent, fadeless and pure,
Here speaks the Comforter, tenderly saying,
"Earth has no sorrow that heaven cannot cure."

3 Here see the bread of life; see waters flowing
Forth from the throne of God, pure from above; [knowing
Come to the feast of love; come, ever
Earth has no sorrow but heaven can remove. [remove.

154. At the Fountain.

OLD MELODY.

CHORUS.

1 Of him who did salvation bring,
I'm at the fountain drinking,
I could forever think and sing,
I'm on my journey home.

CHO —Glory to God,
I'm at the fountain drinking,
Glory to God,
I'm on my journey home.

2 Ask but his grace and lo! 'tis given,
I'm at the fountain drinking,
Ask and he turns your hell to heaven,
I'm on my journey home.

3 Tho' sin and sorrow wound my soul,
I'm at the fountain drinking,
Jesus, thy balm will make me whole,
I'm on my journey home.

4 Where'er I am, where'er I move,
I'm at the fountain drinking,
I meet the object of my love,
I'm on my journey home.

5 Insatiate to this spring I fly,
I'm at the fountain drinking,
I drink and yet am ever dry,
I'm on my journey home.

CHO.—Glory to God,
I'm at the fountain drinking,
Glory to God,
My soul is satisfied.

155 We'll Work till Jesus Comes.

Mrs. Elizabeth Mills. Arr. by W. J. K., 1859. Dr. Wm. Miller.

CHORUS.

1 O land of rest for thee I sigh,
  When will the moment come,
  When I shall lay my armor by
  And dwell in peace at home?

Cho.—We'll work till Jesus comes,
  We'll work till Jesus comes,
  We'll work till Jesus comes,
  And we'll be gather'd home.

2 No tranquil joys on earth I know,
  No peaceful sheltering dome,

This world's a wilderness of woe,
  This world is not my home.

3 To Jesus Christ I fled for rest;
  He bade me cease to roam,
  And lean for succor on his breast
  Till he conduct me home.

4 I sought at once my Saviour's side,
  No more my steps shall roam;
  With him I'll brave death's chilling
  And reach my heavenly home. [tide,

156 Happy Land.

Old Melody.

1. { There is a hap-py land, Far, far a-way.
     Where saints in glory stand. Bright bright as day ; } Oh, how they sweetly sing,

"Worthy is our Saviour King." Loud let his praises ring, Praise, praise for aye!

2 Bright, in that happy land,
  Beams every eye;
  Kept by a Father's hand,
  Love cannot die.
  On, then, to glory run;
  Be a crown and kingdom won;
  And bright, above the sun,
  Reign evermore.

3 Come to that happy land,
  Come, come away;
  Why will you doubting stand?
  Why still delay? ·
  Oh, we shall happy be
  When from sin and sorrow free;
  Lord, we shall dwell with thee,
  Blest evermore.

153

157 **Will You Go?**

Fine.

D.C.

1 We're trav'ling home to heaven above,
    Will you go?
To sing the Saviour's dying love;
    Will you go?
Millions have reached that blest abode,
Anointed kings and priests to God;
And millions more are on the road;
    Will you go?

2 We're going to walk the plains of light,
    Will you go?
Far, far from curse and death and night;
    Will you go?
The crown of life we then shall wear,
The conqueror's palm we then shall bear,
And all the joys of heaven we'll share;
    Will you go?

3 The way to heaven is straight and
    Will you go?   [plain;
Repent, believe, be born again;
    Will you go?
The Saviour cries aloud to thee,
"Take up your cross and follow me,
And thou shalt my salvation see."
    Will you go?

158 **While Jesus Whispers to You.**

WILL. E. WITTER.   H. R. PALMER.

1. While Jesus whispers to you, Come, sinner, come!
   While we are praying for you, Come, ... sin-ner, come!

Now is the time to own him, Come, sinner, come!
Now is the time to know him, Come, ... sin-ner, come!

2 Are you too heavy laden?
    Come, sinner, come!
Jesus will bear your burden,
    Come, sinner, come!
Jesus will not deceive you,
    Come, sinner, come!
Jesus can now redeem you,
    Come, sinner, come!

3 Oh, hear his tender pleading,
    Come, sinner, come!
Come and receive the blessing,
    Come, sinner, come!
While Jesus whispers to you,
    Come, sinner, come!
While we are praying for you,
    Come, sinner, come!

Copyright, 1870, by H. R. Palmer.   154

159

Crown Him.

"Thou hast crowned him with glory and honor."

Rev. Thos. Kelly.   Psalm viii. 5.   Arr. by Geo. G. Stebbins.   By per

Fine.

1. Look, ye saints, the sight is glorious, See the "Man of sorrows" now,
From the fight re-turn vic-to-rious, Ev-'ry knee to him shall bow.
2. Crown the Sav-iour! an-gels crown him, Rich the trophies Jesus brings,
In the seat of power enthrone him, While the vault of heaven rings.

D. C.—Crown him! crown him, angels crown him! Crown the Saviour King of kings.

REFRAIN.

D. C.

Crown him! crown him, angels crown him! Crown the Saviour King of kings;

3 Sinners in derision crowned him,
Mocking thus the Saviour's claim,
Saints and angels crowd around him,
Own his title, praise his name.

4 Hark! the bursts of acclamation!
Hark! these loud, triumphant chords,
Jesus takes the highest station,
Oh, what joy the sight affords!

160 # My Faith Looks Up to Thee.

Ray Palmer.   L. Mason.

1 My faith looks up to thee,
Thou Lamb of Calvary,
Saviour divine!
Now hear me while I pray;
Take all my guilt away;
Oh, let me from this day
Be wholly thine!

2 May thy rich grace impart
Strength to my fainting heart,
My zeal inspire!

As thou hast died for me,
Oh, may my love to thee
Pure, warm, and changeless be—
A living fire!

3 While life's dark maze I tread,
And griefs around me spread,
Be thou my guide;
Bid darkness turn to day,
Wipe sorrow's tears away,
Nor let me ever stray
From thee aside.

4 When ends life's transient dream,
When death's cold sullen stream
Shall o'er me roll,
Blest Saviour! then, in love,
Fear and distrust remove;
Oh, bear me safe above—
A ransomed soul!

161 He is Calling.

FABER. Arr by S. J. VAIL.

1. { There's a wideness in God's mercy, Like the wideness of the sea: }
{ There's a kindness in his justice Which is more than } li - ber-ty.

CHORUS.

He is call-ing, "Come to me!" Lord, I'll gladly haste to thee.

2 There is welcome for the sinner,
   And more graces for the good;
   There is mercy with the Saviour;
   There is healing in his blood.

3 For the love of God is broader
   Than the measure of man's mind;

And the heart of the Eternal
Is most wonderful and kind.

4 If our love were but more simple,
  We should take him at his word;
  And our lives would be all sunshine
  In the sweetness of our Lord.

162 The Golden Key.

"Prayer is the key to unlock the door, and the bolt to shut in the night." J. R. S.

1. Prayer is the key For the bending knee To open the morn's first hours;
2. Not a soul so sad, Nor a heart so glad, When cometh the shades of night,
3. Take the golden key In your hand and see, As the night tide drifts away,

See the incense rise To the star-ry skies, Like per-fume from the flow'rs.
But the daybreak song Will the joy prolong, And some darkness turn to light.
How its blessed hold Is a crown of gold, Thro' the weary hours of day.

4 When the shadows fall,
  And the vesper call
  Is sobbing its low refrain,
  'Tis a garland sweet
  To the toil dent feet,
  And an antidote for pain.

5 Soon the year's dark door
  Shall be shut no more:
  Life's tears shall be wiped away
  As the pearl gates swing,
  And the gold harps ring,
  And the sun unsheathe for aye.

From "Goodly Pearls," by per.

DO RE MI FA SO LA SI

Cleansing Wave.

Mrs. J. F. KNAPP.

CHORUS.

1 OH, now I see the cleansing wave!
  The fountain deed and wide;
Jesus, my Lord, mighty to save,
  Points to his wounded side.

Cho.—The cleansing stream, I see, I see!
  I plunge, and oh, it cleanseth me!
Oh, praise the Lord! it cleanseth me;
  It cleanseth me—yes, cleanseth me.

2 I rise to walk in heaven's own light,
  Above the world of sin,   [white,
With heart made pure and garments
  And Christ enthroned within.

3 Amazing grace! 'tis heaven below
  To feel the blood applied;
And Jesus, only Jesus, know,
  My Jesus crucified.

Doxology.

Words arr. by B. M. A.   Melody by J. R. S.   Harmony by W. J. K.

Slow, with dignity.

Glo - ry be to the FA - THER, Glo - ry be to the SON,

Glo - ry be to the HO - LY GHOST; As it was in the be - ginning,

Is now, and ev - er shall be, World without end. A - men, a - men.

INDEX.

·FINIS·

www.ingramcontent.com/pod-product-compliance
Lightning Source LLC
Chambersburg PA
CBHW030605270326
41927CB00007B/1054